THE
BRIGHT
STUFF

Prentice Hall LIFE

If life is what you make it, then making it better starts here.

What we learn today can change our lives tomorrow. It can change our goals or change our minds; open up new opportunities or simply inspire us to make a difference. That's why we have created a new breed of books that do more to help you make more of *your* life.

Whether you want more confidence or less stress, a new skill or a different perspective, we've designed *Prentice Hall Life* books to help you to make a change for the better. Together with our authors we share a commitment to bring you the brightest ideas and best ways to manage your life, work and wealth.

In these pages we hope you'll find the ideas you need for the life you want. Go on, help yourself.

It's what you make it.

* * *

THE BRIGHT STUFF

Playful ways to nurture your child's extraordinary mind

C.J. Simister

Prentice Hall Life
is an imprint of

PEARSON

Harlow, England • London • New York • Boston • San Francisco • Toronto • Sydney • Singapore • Hong Kong
Tokyo • Seoul • Taipei • New Delhi • Cape Town • Madrid • Mexico City • Amsterdam • Munich • Paris • Milan

Pearson Education Limited

Edinburgh Gate
Harlow CM20 2JE
Tel: +44 (0)1279 623623
Fax: +44 (0)1279 431059
Website: www.pearsoned.co.uk

First published in Great Britain in 2009

ISBN: 978-0-273-72817-7

British Library Cataloguing-in-Publication Data
A catalogue record for this book is available from the British Library

Library of Congress Cataloging-in-Publication Data
Simister, C. J.
    The bright stuff : playful ways to nurture your child's extraordinary mind / CJ Simister.
        p. cm.
    Includes bibliographical references.
    ISBN 978-0-273-72817-7 (pbk.)
    1. Education–Parent participation. 2. Home and school. 3. Activity programs in education. 4. Academic achievement. I. Title.
    LB1048.5.S58 2009
    371.19'2–dc22

                    2009025892

The publisher is grateful to J. K. Rowling for permission to reproduce the quote on page 216 from *Harry Potter and the Chamber of Secrets*. Copyright © J. K. Rowling 1998.

Mind Map® is a registered trademark of the Buzan Organisation Limited 1990. For more information, contact: BUZAN CENTRES WORLDWIDE PLC, www.buzancentresworldwide.com

10 9 8 7 6
13

Text design by Design Deluxe
Typeset in ClassGaramond BT 11 pt by 3
Printed and bound in Great Britain by Ashford Colour Press, Gosport, Hants

The publisher's policy is to use paper manufactured from sustainable forests.

*Dedicated to the children of Northwood College,
whose enthusiasm for games and activities that develop
independent thinking has shown me what a powerful
difference we – as parents and teachers – can make.*

CONTENTS

ABOUT THE AUTHOR

C. J. Simister directs a highly innovative thinking skills programme that prepares children for the rapidly changing and challenging world they will face beyond the scope of school tests and exams. The success of this programme has led to ongoing requests to discuss and demonstrate her techniques at national and international conferences and workshops for children, teachers and parents. She has 14 years' experience of teaching children of all ages in both independent and state schools, an economics degree (University of Cambridge) and an MA in school improvement (London's Institute of Education).

She is the author of several books and papers, including a book for schools called *How to Teach Thinking and Learning Skills: A Practical Programme for the Whole School* (Paul Chapman Publishing: 2007). A firm believer that the least constructive thing to do with a hoop is to jump through it, she hopes that, by teaching children to think for themselves, the future could still be bright.

INTRODUCTION

A bright future for your child: The hidden secrets of success

Your children will learn an enormous amount at school. It may not always, unfortunately, translate into the very best grades or the perfect report card (if only that were the case!), but that doesn't mean it's not vast.

Aside from the many different subjects they'll encounter – the science and technology, the English and maths, the history, geography and religious studies and so on – your children will learn practical skills to help them keep fit, healthy and safe, to express themselves through art, drama and music, and, as if they needed it, the technological know-how to ensure that their supreme position within the household as head of all that is computer-related is never even remotely called into question.

But that's not all. They will also find out about the importance of accuracy and attention to detail, of following instructions carefully, of managing time and working to a deadline. True, it would be a tad unrealistic to say that each child will become a world expert at all these things, but there will at least be plenty of opportunities to practise them.

Together with this are all the social and emotional skills involved in learning to get along with their peers and teachers, not to mention coming to recognise their position in a wider community – and, wherever it can be squeezed into what's already a pretty jam-packed schedule, your children will also be taught about values such as honesty, integrity, respect and tolerance.

At the end of all of this, we trust that the product will be children who will emerge happy, fulfilled and ready to achieve their full potential in life. Oh – and with the all-important set of certificates that are supposed to attest to their effort and intelligence, to demonstrate their readiness for college or their first job.

No wonder schools are busy places.

Surely there is just no more space in the timetable to add yet more demands. But the thing is, this massive list still contains an even more massive gap – and one that's becoming ever more glaring in today's unpredictable and rapidly changing world. Increasingly, there are *other ingredients* that are needed if children are truly to flourish, to shine and to become all they can be.

And we know this must be the case! Many of us – both teachers and parents – are more than a little uncomfortable about the fact that years are spent filling children's heads with all sorts of facts and figures that – if we're honest and if our kids are anything like us – will probably be forgotten pretty much as soon as the exams are over. Alongside this, we have an uneasy sense that children are looking rather ill-equipped to face today's big, bad (but tremendously exciting) world and really show it who's boss.

The cracks are already starting to show when it comes to higher education. Otherwise, how could it be that a student can leave school with nothing but A grades and still not receive a single interview for their chosen course at university? Why are universities doing back-flips to find new ways of selecting students – resorting to entrance tests that test 'thinking', combing through personal statements for 'that elusive something that sets a candidate apart from the A-grade uniformity' (Tahir, 2008) and asking interview questions that have apparently included 'Tell me about a banana'?

The answer is simple. Sure, a good school education matters. *But it's not enough.*

The fundamental secrets of success are *qualities*. Drawing on the observations of philosophers, writers, scientists and entrepreneurs, this book brings together 16 characteristics that will influence not only a child's achievement but also their whole life for the better. Things such as:

- the instinct to persist when the going gets tough;
- the self-belief to come up with new, innovative and potentially transforming ideas;
- the patience to stop, reflect and make decisions wisely in the face of unforeseen dilemmas;
- the ability to think laterally and find surprising solutions to awkward problems;
- the willingness to approach issues with an open, astute mind;
- the courage to take a gamble when the moment is right, and the sheer bloody-mindedness to get back up and try again when you fail.

The trouble is, there's simply no space on the syllabus for this stuff in most schools.

Too often, even the brightest children are led blindly into the 'repeat after me' trap. The reality for schools is that they are judged by the achievement of their pupils. Since the most reliable way to secure good grades is to play it safe, then you can understand the decision that too often follows: stick closely to the curriculum, teach exactly what's needed and force-feed children with the information required to waddle through hoops.

The result is that kids may look savvy – but scratch the surface and too frequently you find stunted creativity, a lack of rigour and minimal independent thought. Children learn to research and regurgitate other people's ideas and opinions but not to generate their own. When taken out of the narrow scope of their GCSE and A level subjects, they're at a loss – with few strategies at hand to make thoughtful decisions and little experience of forming balanced opinions. Some schools are trying hard to fight against this, but too often the environment our kids are growing up in, the one that is forming their beliefs and behaviours, is one that suppresses genuine thinking in favour of conforming, memorising, repeating – getting it right rather than truly getting it.

> This problem isn't new. The sixteenth-century French philosopher Montaigne wrote: 'I gladly come back to the theme of the absurdity of our education: its end has not been to make us good and wise but learned ... We ought to find out not who understands most but who understands best ... We work merely to fill the memory' (quoted by de Botton, 2000).
>
> And still earlier, the ancient Greek philosopher Heraclitus noted: 'Knowing many things doesn't teach insight.'

This chimes with Malcolm Gladwell's observation, in his bestselling book *Outliers: The Story of Success*, that, in fact, those people with the highest IQ are not necessarily life's big achievers. Rather, it is the presence or absence of other qualities such as innovation, creativity and persistence, coupled with the willingness to work hard (not to mention a helping of luck), that really makes the difference. He distinguishes between the sort of *convergent* thinking used to find the right answer in abstract IQ-type tests and the *divergent* thinking required to write down as many different uses as you can for a brick and a blanket. Gladwell argues that the latter has a much greater chance of predicting future success: it is the candidate with the 'fertile mind', the one with imagination, creativity and lateral thinking, who is most likely to thrive.

Part of you may still be wondering what all the fuss is about. For many people, a conventional education seems to have done just fine. And so it's worth saying again: the world is changing. Even if a conventional education was sufficient before, it may not be in the future. No one can predict what the next 10 years will hold, let alone the next 50 or 100. One of those random but intriguing statistics gaining credence purely from its appearance on multiple websites is that 60 per cent of the jobs that our children will do have not yet even been invented. We don't know how this figure was ever calculated. We do know, however, that turning out a steady stream of non-thinking, non-dreaming, non-grappling young people – even if they've a whole string of A levels – is not only wasting their real potential but is also horribly short-sighted.

A powerful role for parents

When they are very young, children have extraordinary minds. Whether it is their elaborate imagination with its capacity for inventing brave new worlds, their unfailing curiosity in everything around them or those unexpected, quirky ideas that make us stop and ask, 'Why did I never think of that?', one of the joys of being a parent or a teacher is that children so often surprise and amaze us.

What a tragedy then that conformity tends gradually to replace creativity, asking the big questions turns into seeking an acceptable answer, and risk-aversion (in our increasingly paranoid culture) replaces a sense of adventure. In the end, too often the box wins and we forget how we ever thought outside it. The outcome is school-leavers who lack the skills needed to flourish in a rapidly changing world – by fitting in, they become less likely ever to stand out.

But this needn't be the case. The crucial thing is that this curiosity and inventiveness is not allowed to seep away. And the best-placed people to see that this happens are you, the parents. There are all sorts of techniques that you can introduce to your children as soon as they can talk. Taking one secret of success at a time, this book describes a wealth of wonderful activities and games that mums and dads can call on, to preserve, nurture, grow and enhance that early creative potential in their children.

During the early years, the plasticity of the brain – its capacity to 'grow' skills, values and behaviours that will later become habits – is at its peak. Making even small changes to the way you talk and play with your child can have a real impact. It's cognitive development – but without the smart pills.

The ideas are designed to fit in with everyday family life, involving little or no preparation. They're perfect for keeping children amused in spare moments – over a meal, in the car or even when stuck in the queue at the super-market – while at the same time fostering their investigative spirit, encouraging determination and initiative, and demonstrating that failure can be a useful springboard for the next step forward.

This book is intended to be a very practical dip-in guide. The activities described are aimed at children within the 4–16 years age range: they deliberately don't have more precise ages attached because children aren't like that. You know your child better than anyone else does. Pick out a few ideas and try them. If they work, that's great – stick with them. If they don't, it doesn't matter – try adapting them or simply put them to one side; they may work better if you return to them at a later stage. You're likely to find that some of the simplest ideas may prove the most effective – and that, with a little tweaking, many of these games will be enjoyed by children of any age.

You will quickly spot which of the qualities described here are ones your kids already have a real flair for. It might surprise you! You'll also be in the best position to notice the gaps. For some, it might be a reluctance to take a risk and try new things; for others, it might be a tendency to give up too quickly or an unwillingness to develop their own ideas and views. It may be that you're wondering how to help your children show greater initiative when they face tricky situations or how to encourage them to be less gullible and more worldly-wise when deciding for themselves who and what to believe.

Whether it's nurturing those early hidden talents that are so often overlooked (but that are likely to be of far more importance to them in the end than a particular grade in a particular examination) or filling the gaps by supporting your child with the things he or she finds hard, as parents you have a fantastic opportunity to make a real difference. With your help, your child has a real chance of growing just the sort of skills and qualities that will give them every opportunity to flourish and make the most of life's opportunities.

As well as turning to some of the greatest minds in history for insights, this book draws on extensive research and a wide range of sources – some of which will sound familiar to anyone who has undergone training as an adult in creative thinking, decision analysis or different styles of learning.

Parents often express real excitement at discovering that these things could become an integral part of their children's experience – rather than tacked on years later when we've already a host of learnt behaviours to unpick and overcome. A common reaction at workshops is: 'I wish I'd been introduced to this when I was young!'

It is also the product of the fascinating experience of working at an unusually forward-looking school where learning to think independently is truly on the curriculum; a school that has determined to address the problem that Sir Ken Robinson, author of the bestselling *Out of Our Minds*, flagged up, that 'we now have a school curriculum that teaches ten subjects but only limited ways of thinking'.

Most of all, however, this book emerges from many hours spent in the company of children – watching them struggle, watching them triumph and watching them glow with pride when they realise that they can, after all, think amazingly well for themselves. It's a great experience for a teacher. But it must be even more rewarding for a parent.

I'm not sure I need this - my child thinks already!

The wealth of ideas in this book is intended to boost what you are almost certainly doing instinctively. Many parents will already be encouraging their kids to be curious about the world in which they live and to have a go at guessing why things work the way they work; they will of course be helping them to make good decisions and encouraging them to stick with things when they're hard.

Nevertheless, it's quite easy to be fooled by how well kids seem to be doing. Many are seemingly very successfully steering their way through school and won't discover until later how many important gaps there have been.

Here's a quick check-list of the traits most commonly mistaken for effective thinking, along with a few short-cuts to suggested ideas and activities that might help if the description sounds at all familiar.

Six things that look like thinking

1 The distant stare

Some children just happen to *look* like they're thinking. This may reflect any number of things, from boredom to hunger to complete confusion! It's certainly no guarantee that quality thinking is taking place.

What's more, just because a child daydreams a lot doesn't automatically mean he or she is building up a wonderful and creative imagination. Certainly, time spent drifting in seemingly random thoughts can be valuable – but learning to use a rudder is helpful too.

> You could try . . .
> ◄■ How to encourage originality and creativity: p. 93
> ◄■ How to become innovative and inventive: p. 109
> . . . for suggested activities to help children pin down and direct their own thinking.

2 The steady stream of questions

There's no denying that asking questions can be a good thing – but, as every parent will know, there are different sorts of questions. A steady stream of the 'Are we nearly there?' type doesn't prove your child's got an enquiring mind.

There are *layers* of questions, starting with closed questions that require a simple factual response, moving up through those that seek to challenge and deepen understanding, to peak with those wonderful, rare questions that test the boundaries of what is currently accepted – where some serious thinking is needed to explore a range of possible and perhaps hypothetical ideas.

It's worth looking more carefully at the type of questions our children are asking. More often than not, they take their cues from the adults around them. Might we accidentally be teaching them to ask questions where they gain credit simply for accumulating a growing pile of bland factual knowledge?

> You could try . . .
>
> ━▬ How to kindle a burning curiosity: p. 59
>
> ━▬ How to develop a 'let's find out' approach: p. 71
>
> . . . for suggested activities to help children learn to ask 'thinking questions' and to follow them up with their own investigations.

3 The know-it-all

It's easy to learn a few facts (names of trees or capital cities, dates of battles and so on) and then bring them out when you need to impress someone. If children see that this is what's valued, then some will get it down to a fine art. But thinking is not about labelling things. It's about grappling, constructing, realigning.

As the French philosopher Descartes said, 'It is not enough to have a good mind, the main thing is to use it well'. Don't be fooled by the child who seems to know it all but panics when out of his or her thinking comfort zone.

You could try . . .

➡ How to sort sense from nonsense: p. 177

➡ How to take the right sort of risk: p. 145

. . . for suggested activities that help develop critical thinking skills and an adventurous spirit.

4 The hard worker – neat writing and good grades

On the surface it seems that our children are 'working' harder than ever before – juggling homework from the age of five, taking tests at every level and learning the meaning of stress years before we'd ever heard of the word. But, as mentioned earlier, look a little deeper and you often find they've simply been trained to absorb and regurgitate – the school's safe route to exam success. This is a far cry from developing the confidence, resilience and creativity to form innovative ideas and theories that will take us forward on a *new* path, rather than merely summarising where we've already been.

It is important that students bring a certain ragamuffin barefoot irreverence to their studies; they are not here to worship what is known, but to question it. Jacob Bronowski

Research has shown this may be a particular problem for bright girls. Girls who do well at school sometimes reveal – when probed a little more deeply – surprisingly low self-confidence and resilience (Dweck, 2000). Their motivation is tied too closely to pleasing others – they judge themselves by the reaction gained from their latest piece of work rather than from a belief in themselves as a skilled learner and thinker. This means they are poorly placed to cope with failure and tend to avoid situations that might challenge them. Instead of trying something new, they are effectively being trained to believe that it's safer to repeat – neatly and succinctly, of course – the thoughts of other people, whose ideas have already been met with approval.

You could try . . .

➡ How to stimulate independent thinking: p. 3

➡ How to develop initiative and forward thinking: p. 269

. . . for suggested activities that help develop an active, independent mind.

5 The 'knows their own mind' type

In this case, it all depends on how the opinions got there in the first place. If they have been formed as a result of careful deliberation, weighing up the options and listening to all the evidence, then great! (And, by the way, please mention to your child the benefits of a career in politics.)

However, a hotly held position may simply be the product of an irrational gut instinct or it might be a copy of or a reaction against the view held by a favourite or least favourite figure of authority (parent, teacher, rap artist, footballer . . .). Indeed, there's a lot to be said for having weaker opinions if it means you stay open to new ideas and information.

You could try . . .

➡ How to think flexibly: p. 201

➡ How to make wise decisions: p. 217

. . . for suggested activities to encourage different perspectives and novel connections.

6 The avid reader

This one's placed deliberately at the end, because reading is such a wonderful thing that I'm reluctant to risk undermining it. Reading can open the mind to new ideas, heighten the imagination, improve concentration and focus, enhance empathy – not to mention develop vital literacy skills. But – and here it has to come – it does depend on the choice of reading material. The equivalent of chicklit and car magazines is increasingly finding its way on to school library shelves and – while they may be good for the reluctant reader, in which case it's all about seeking *anything* that will provide a way in – this sort of easy reading is not necessarily doing much for a child's thinking.

What's more, the value gained from reading is very different if you skim through a book quickly as opposed to letting it dwell in your mind, probing the story line, questioning motives and exploring the ideas. Let's just say that reading avidly is a great place to start – but 'reading for thinking' is something that may need a little nudging.

> You could try . . .
> How to grow a vivid imagination: p. 21
> . . . for suggested activities to encourage deeper thinking about stories.

what to aim for

Drawing on the wisdom of philosophers, writers, scientists and entrepreneurs, it seems clear that it is certain qualities – or *thinking habits* – that make the real difference to a person's future, regardless of what career they choose or direction they follow. We need to be raising children who:

- **Are curious** – who genuinely enjoy collecting ideas and discovering new things, who show an interest in what's going on in the world, who ask big, open-ended questions, who engage with moral and philosophical issues and are not content with a simple answer.

- **Are astute** – questioning what they hear, gathering different opinions and weighing the pros and cons of various options, reasoning logically and sorting the sense from the nonsense before deciding what to believe.

- **Are creative with their thoughts rather than thinking within conventional boundaries** – who enjoy forming and expressing their own explanations and theories, who play with ideas rather than fixing on the first right answer that comes along, and who make connections, building upon what they know and applying it to different situations.

- **Are brave** – enjoying new challenges and sticking with it when learning seems hard, who stand by a reasoned opinion regardless of other people's reactions and who understand when it's worth taking a risk and trying something new.

- **Are rigorous** – who persist until they're really satisfied with what they have discovered or decided, and who are willing to refine and improve their own ideas, learning from successes and failures and seeking help when it's needed.

- **Are open-minded** – willing to learn from other

people and to share points of view, who recognise that new ideas and plans are sometimes better formed by pooling talents, and who are able to switch perspective and adapt when new evidence is presented or if the situation changes.

- **Are able to laugh at themselves and keep a balanced perspective** – understanding that mistakes happen and knowing how to pick themselves up again afterwards.

- **Are resourceful and independent** – who show initiative and set goals for themselves, accepting responsibility for the direction they choose to take.

This may sound idealistic, but it's far from it. In fact, it's both liberating and wonderfully equalising for children. These traits are not the normal stuff of tests and trauma. They are eminently achievable, within reach – and, what's more, they're fun to reach for.

For me, one of the most rewarding aspects of developing a school initiative that nurtures these sorts of qualities has been to see children, some of whom perhaps weren't so great at the more traditional 'school skills', gain enormous satisfaction and confidence from discovering that they are particularly talented at asking seriously good questions, at recognising an adult's illogical conclusion or at coming up with a whole list of innovative suggestions. How fantastic to discover that they have the potential to dream up ideas that no one else has thought of before – many of which will no doubt lead nowhere, but one of which – when further developed – might be a real winner! To be instilled with the confidence and skills to tackle any situation that arises – not because they know it all (in fact, how reassuring to discover this isn't necessary) but because they *know what to do with their not knowing*, a phrase coined by Guy Claxton, creator of 'Building Learning Power'.

Traditional education doesn't offer many opportunities for these sorts of talents to grow, so they often lie dormant or – worse – wither away undiscovered.

> By emphasising the sort of qualities listed here, the aim is to steer children away from the belief that a successful future is limited to those who are conventionally 'clever'. The message of this book is that we can help *all* children – regardless of ability in the traditional sense – to develop the characteristics and confidence that will help them to thrive, whatever direction they choose to take.

Three top tips

1 Model everything, including the mistakes!

It's a slightly discomfiting thought, but children watch adults very closely – particularly their parents. They pick up your language, your mannerisms and your attitudes. This means that the first and most important piece of advice is that you do your best to model for them the sort of characteristics that are described.

One way of doing this is to get involved yourself with the activities. Introduce them as excellent new games that you've just come across and that you're eager to try yourself. You'll demonstrate that stretching one's thinking is something that can be fun for everyone, and your child will love the fact that, with these sorts of exercises, it won't always be the grown-up who has the best idea.

What's more, if you're anything like me, you may also notice your own thinking improving along the way . . .

2 Use praise to encourage big progress, not a big head

It's very often the case that children will live up (or down) to other people's expectations of them. Self-belief is hugely determined by our perception of how other people view us.

This has the rather staggering implication that you can make all the difference in the world to your children simply by believing in them. Believe that they are creative and great at generating imaginative ideas. Believe that they are always the ones to come up with the interesting question and to make the unexpected observation. Believe that they are fantastic at making wise decisions in tricky situations. Believe that they are skilled problem-solvers, frequently able to come up with a novel solution that you wouldn't have thought of. Believe that – when these things don't happen – it's just that they are still developing, still learning, still trying, *not* that you've misjudged them.

Your belief will rub off on them. It will, quite literally, help them to grow up as extraordinary thinking children who will, one day, become extraordinary thinking adults.

But here's the tricky bit. An easy mistake to make is to place such emphasis on building up confidence that the necessary counter-balances of rigour and humility are overlooked. Admiring and praising *everything* your child says is likely to leave you with an overconfident, smug little horror who thinks that what they've got to say is more valuable than what anyone else has to offer.

A balance needs to be found. Your children are right at the beginning of their development as independent thinkers – and, as a result, their ideas, suggestions and theories need to be treated with the greatest of care. A ruthless assessment of their worth compared with an adult's fully thought through theory will put them off for life. A bland 'well done, darling' will nurture complacency and certainly won't promote the sort of qualities you're hoping your child will develop.

Here are a couple of suggestions for how to tackle this dilemma.

Focus mostly on praising the *qualities*, rather than the outcomes

Remember that you're trying to teach your child that using their brain is fun – it's an adventure – and that it's not what they immediately come out with that matters anywhere near as much as the fact that they've got their brain fully turned on in the first place. Here are a few of the sort of replies that can be used:

- It's really good that you've thought about two/several different options there. Just talk me through them again ...
- I'm impressed that you've tried to grapple with that. It's a difficult one isn't it? It's good that you're trying to think it through properly – lots of people would just settle for a quick answer.
- Well done – you're certainly thinking laterally! That's an idea I'd never have thought of. Tell me more about how it would work ...

- That's great – you've really kept working on your idea, haven't you? It's sounding much more realistic/imaginative/possible now. What did you change? Do you think you could make it any better, or do you reckon that's it now?

- You're great at coming up with ideas! OK – tell me its plus points. Can you come up with the same number of minus points? So what's your final decision? Or have you begun to think of an even better idea?

Be specific with your praise

When your child comes up with an idea, *listen* to it. Although the focus should mostly be on praising the *act* of thinking, sometimes there really will be something of value in what they say. For example, they may have:

- made a good decision, having weighed up the options;
- worked out a clever solution to a difficult problem;
- come up with a really unusual and imaginative idea.

Remember that, for much of the time, children are unlikely to think of any truly innovative ideas that people with greater experience and expertise haven't come up with. It's up to you to make a judgement as to whether their idea is particularly creative, given their age, ability, track record, etc. This isn't something to worry about – you'll know when your child surprises you! In these cases, you have the lovely task of looking truly impressed and commenting specifically on what it was about their idea that was so fantastic.

Stay relaxed: start young, start small

Even if you pick only a handful of the ideas in this book, you'll be making a difference. Family life is quite frantic enough already without taking on too much all at once. This isn't a quick-fix solution. This book represents an ongoing approach to raising a child that will work best if infused into what you do over many years. You're in a wonderful position because your child will be with you for such a long time: you can start young and start small.

How does the rest of this book work?

Taking one secret of success at a time, the next 16 chapters offer practical advice, hints, activities and games to help parents fill in those vital gaps in a child's development.

A guide to the symbols used

A variety of symbols are used to help you navigate your way around this book:

And another thought!

 Extra tips and references that may prove useful.

School link

Ideas for how to support your child's thinking about school subjects. This is *not* because children need to do yet more work – rather, the idea is simply that children are likely to enjoy topics more and find them of greater relevance if they feel that people at home are also interested in finding out about them.

For the deeper thinker

More challenging ideas for children who show a particular interest.

Given that none of us has as much time as we'd like, the 'Short-cuts' section below offers a quick guide to selecting the best activities to fit in with a hectic schedule.

Short-cuts

1 Star activities: where to start if you're pushed for time

For those of you whose busy lifestyle means you start to laugh hysterically at the thought of reading this book from start to finish, I hope the following table may be of some help. In it, I have listed a selection of activities that, in my experience, are absolute winners. They always work and they're always popular. If you try these, you'll be making a fantastic start.

2 Stuck in a traffic jam? Ideas for specific situations

This is the place to look if you've got a particular situation coming up and you'd like to dip in to the book and pick out two or three activities to have up your sleeve. If you run out, remember that lots of other games in the book would fit these situations too.

Out shopping

Car journeys

Diamond thinking (p. 18)

Magic questions (p. 28)

It's a wacky world (p. 54)

Finger questions (p. 68)

Magic powder (p. 68)

Alternative uses (p. 99)

Rubbish! (p. 100)

20 ways ... (p. 101)

Connect – disconnect! (p. 102)

What was the question? (p. 102)

Loony logic (p. 105)

Flog it! (p. 106)

Magic eye pictures (p. 133)

Concentrate! (p. 133)

On the bright side ... (p. 134)

Picture this! (p. 210)

I've got a problem ... (p. 221)

Just suppose ... (p. 224)

Your challenge is to ... (p. 242)

Mystery routes (p. 243)

The great outdoors

Everyday mysteries (p. 29)

Clouds (p. 31)

Five things you spot about ... (p. 42)

Tune in! (p. 50)

Blind man's journey (p. 51)

Making up new games (p. 119)

Odd one out (p. 206)

It's a mystery! (p. 209)

Switch! (p. 213)

Walking adventures (p. 284)

At an art gallery or museum

What's in a picture? (p. 30)

Five things you spot about ... (p. 42)

What's always true about ...? (p. 45)

Open eyes, open mind (p. 185)

Odd one out (p. 206)

Quiet afternoons

At the table

Parties		
Memory pictures (p. 43) Spot the difference (p. 44)	All ears (p. 53) Think 'n' run (p. 211)	Tied up in knots! (p. 244)

Bedtime		
Magic questions (p. 28) What's in a picture? (p. 30) Story questions (p. 32) Imagine if ... (p. 33)	How many ways ...? (p. 34) The memory walk (p. 56) Persistence role models (p. 138)	The patchwork game (p. 207) CTB: creative thinking backwards (p. 240) CTF: creative thinking forwards (p. 241)

3 Suggested activities to help with common problems

Every child is unique and you, of all people, will know exactly what your own child's strengths are. You're also likely to have a few nagging worries – because loving parents always do. Perhaps your daughter is shy and finds it hard to communicate with other people. Maybe your son seems rather easily led and you wish he would stop to think for himself.

If so, the tables opposite may help you to identify activities that could be worth trying as a first port of call to help tackle that particular issue.

Lots of interesting thoughts, but tends to keep them to him- or herself

Just a minute (p. 17)

Everyday mysteries (p. 29)

What's in a picture? (p. 30)

Story questions (p. 32)

Make a wonder walk (p. 66)

Magic powder (p. 68)

News time (p. 88)

Concept collages (p. 104)

I am like a ... (p. 107)

Good side, bad side (p. 169)

What do you believe but cannot prove? (p. 187)

The patchwork game (p. 207)

Just suppose ... (p. 224)

Team tasks (p. 265)

What do I want? (p. 285)

Less confident of own ideas, preferring to be led and told what to think

Philosophy at home (p. 14)

Story questions (p. 32)

Loony logic (p. 105)

One idea sparks another ... (p. 118)

Keep a risk record (p. 155)

Taking risks with food (p. 157)

Shock statistics (p. 189)

Advert alert! (p. 194)

Product packaging (p. 196)

Picture this! (p. 210)

Thinking friends (p. 236)

Role play (p. 263)

Team tasks (p. 264)

In the control seat (p. 284)

Walking adventures (p. 284)

Heaps of energy, but finds it hard to concentrate

Five things you spot about ... (p. 42)

Memory pictures (p. 43)

Spot the difference (p. 44)

This and that (p. 46)

Mix 'n' match (p. 48)

Tune in! (p. 50)

All ears (p. 53)

It's a wacky world (p. 54)

The memory walk (p. 56)

Investigation journal (p. 77)

Go shop! (p. 115)

Magic eye pictures (p. 133)

Construction and balancing games (p. 135)

Su dokus (p. 186)

Mystery routes (p. 243)

Logical and practical – but not very imaginative

The squiggle game (p. 27)

Hidden treasures (p. 27)

What's in a picture? (p. 30)

Imagine if . . . (p. 33)

The 'What if . . .?' game (p. 64)

Alternative uses (p. 99)

Rubbish! (p. 100)

20 ways . . . (p. 101)

Someone else's shoes (p. 101)

Improve it (p. 115)

Into the future (p. 119)

Imagine that . . . (p. 120)

On the bright side . . . (p. 134)

It's a mystery! (p. 209)

Random-input problem-solving (p. 250)

Hesitant and unsure about making decisions

Diamond thinking (p. 18)

This and that (p. 46)

Magic powder (p. 68)

Secret science (p. 83)

Keep a risk record (p. 155)

Good side, bad side (p. 169)

The uncertainty spectrum (p. 182)

Think 'n' run (p. 211)

Switch! (p. 213)

The big question is . . . (p. 213)

I've got a problem . . . (p. 221)

Trading places (p. 222)

Tug of war (p. 224)

Reverse thinking (p. 226)

Your challenge is to . . . (p. 242)

Full of ideas, but needs to stop and think things through more deeply

Digging deeper (p. 13)

Tell me about a banana (p. 15)

What's always true about . . .? (p. 45)

Newsround (p. 90)

What was the question? (p. 102)

Crazy connections (p. 103)

Guess what? (p. 184)

Crazy conclusions (p. 185)

The great problem-solving machine (p. 238)

CTB: creative thinking backwards (p. 240)

CTF: creative thinking forwards (p. 241)

Flow diagrams (p. 245)

Real-life lateral thinking (p. 248)

Practical problem-solving (p. 249)

Follow my lead (p. 282)

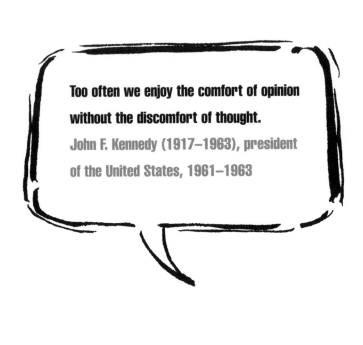

Too often we enjoy the comfort of opinion without the discomfort of thought.

John F. Kennedy (1917–1963), president of the United States, 1961–1963

HOW TO STIMULATE INDEPENDENT THINKING

The most important place to start. We all want our children to think for themselves. We want them to learn to develop interesting ideas and to form their own thoughtful and balanced opinions. Most likely, we also want them to grow up to be able to talk about these clearly and confidently, unfazed by whatever situation or audience they face.

It's surprisingly tricky stuff though – and, despite what we might think, this is not something that necessarily happens automatically. While there are always some kids who seem to be born with a natural ability to discuss their thoughts openly with whoever's at hand, this is often the result of a very particular type of upbringing. Far more common is the child who, despite all of his or her achievements at school, is reduced to a string of half-formed or merely repeated ideas when faced with an adult who has asked his or her opinion.

The thing is, most children are only really used to talking to their friends, family and teachers. And subjects are often limited to the day-to-day or the curriculum – leaving little scope for the sort of topic that really stimulates some serious independent thought. No wonder even the brightest sometimes freeze when faced with a new situation like an interview or other encounter with someone who might make a real difference to their future.

It takes a lot of time and encouragement to help a child grow a genuine confidence in their own thinking and speaking. Newly forming opinions are unlikely to be perfect – they need to be nurtured, tested and adjusted. The easiest thing in the world is to put a child off by telling them *what* to think, rather than gently supporting them in learning to think for themselves.

But those who do so have a massive advantage. For a start, we often judge a person's intelligence by their ability to talk clearly and confidently. A young person who knows that he or she is quite capable of thinking through the issues related to whatever topic is thrown at them is, quite literally, empowered. They come across as having a natural sense that they are worthy of inclusion in adult conversation, something that tends to be self-fulfilling. They are also more likely to volunteer for new opportunities, develop new skills and make new contacts. From the start, they are paving the way for a successful future.

This means that one of the most important pieces of advice that can be given to any parent is – quite simply – to talk about things. This section offers several practical suggestions for how to help your child to form their own early opinions and how to give them the confidence to communicate these with a range of audiences.

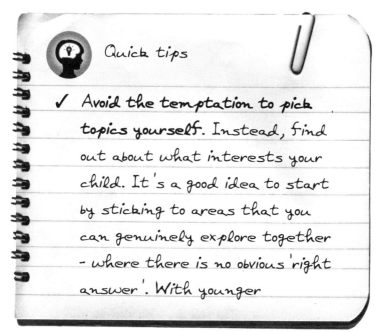

Quick tips

✓ Avoid the temptation to pick topics yourself. Instead, find out about what interests your child. It's a good idea to start by sticking to areas that you can genuinely explore together – where there is no obvious 'right answer'. With younger children, the sort of imaginative topics raised by their own questions are ideal (see Chapter 4 for practical ideas). Older children are often extremely interested in all sorts of wider moral or hypothetical issues – they just may not show this at home for fear of the lecture that will ensue. Try 'Philosophy at home' (p. 14) for a few suggestions.

✓ **Look out for times that suit your child to talk about these sorts of issues.** Remember that children are often very tired by the end of the evening, so earlier in the day is usually better. You could, for example, have a 'food-for-thought lunch' or a 'tea-time talk' once a week when everyone brings along something they'd like to chat about.

✓ Show that you are excited about the topic and that you're looking forward to exploring the sorts of ideas and opinions that you and your child might come up with together. Hold fire on giving too many of your own answers, and instead use the opportunity to find out what your child thinks. Remember that the most common mistake made by enthusiastic parents is that a discussion quickly becomes an occasion to impart wisdom rather than a two-way debate.

✓ **Don't forget that your children are younger than you!** They haven't had a chance to develop skills of critical thinking and argument and don't have anywhere near as much knowledge at their finger tips. Even if you feel strongly that your child's suggestions are naive or even wrong, it's vital that you don't make your child feel silly for saying them. A good discussion will provide genuine opportunities for children to scrutinise, to speculate and

to develop their own tentative.
ideas and theories. Your main
task is, therefore, to help
them feel that their ideas
are of value. Listen to them.
Point out what's interesting or
original about what they say
and then gently probe their
understanding and reasoning
with questions such as these:
- So what would you say to a
  person who listened to all
  of that, but still felt that
  ...?
- What would you tell them
  was good about their idea?
- This is getting really fascinating! Do you think anyone
  else might have a different
  opinion? What might they
  say? Do you disagree with

all or just some of those points? Could you use any of them to make your own argument even better?

– So, where are we now on this? We've covered so many interesting points that my head is spinning! Can you sum up our final conclusion in one sentence for me?

✓ Help your child learn that changing their mind during a discussion is absolutely fine. Tell them it's a sign of real intelligence if someone listens to what another person has to say, decides that some or all of it is more convincing than their own position, and then adjusts their view accordingly. For little ones, an easy way to get this point across is to talk about having a 'bendy brain'!

✓ By all means, drop in your own ideas and bits of background information - but try to do so in a way that shows that these are things you've been thinking about which you've discovered and found fascinating, rather than as corrections or lessons. Remember that, all the time, your aim is to help your child to become an idea developer - you're encouraging him or her to play the central role of thinker.

✓ An obvious final point, but really important - children who grow up with busy, full households are far more likely to develop a natural social confidence and ability to talk about a range of topics with all sorts of people: something that will be of enormous benefit throughout their life. If possible, invite people round - as diverse a selection as you can - and, from an early age, develop the expectation that your child(ren) will join in with the conversation, at least for part of the time.

Activities and games

You could try . . .

DIGGING DEEPER

This extremely simple pattern is one that you've probably found yourself using many times. It can be used when discussing all sorts of subjects and is great for developing the sort of mind that won't be thrown by unexpected, very open-ended questions. It also helps your child to form opinions that are backed up by quality reasoning.

- What do you think about this story/picture/ photograph? (Ideally pick something in which your child has already shown an interest.)
- Why do you think that . . . ? Why? Why?

It's important to repeat the 'why' two or three times, where appropriate, to bring your child's reasoning to the surface. Keep this activity light-hearted and fun, so that it's a game rather than an interrogation! Younger children find it very funny being asked 'why?' several times and so tend to enjoy this activity. You'll see from their struggle, however, that opinions are rarely based upon genuine reasoning, emerging instead from instinct or half-thought-through ideas. With time, practice and encouragement, this should change.

PHILOSOPHY AT HOME

It's been reported that a degree in philosophy is increasingly sought after by employers, who find that the skills of analytical and innovative thinking involved are extremely useful (Shepherd, 2007). While this is certainly one way of improving one's ability to think independently, just imagine the benefits for a child who develops these sorts of approaches right from the very start.

Suggested philosophical topics might include:

- Where does everything come from?
- Are humans different from animals? If so, how?
- Is it always right to tell the truth?
- What is the difference between good and bad?
- If you borrow something and forget to give it back, is it stealing?
- How do we know we're alive and not in someone else's dream?
- What does it mean to be free? Should we all have a free will? Is freedom of speech a good thing?
- What is happiness/sadness/friendship made of?
- Is there life elsewhere?

And a slightly morbid, but fascinating one for older children:

- If you could choose what would be written on your gravestone, what would it be? Why?

Ask your child for more such ideas – it's likely that they'll come up with far more than you!

TELL ME ABOUT A BANANA

Based on a question that legend has it was asked at an Oxbridge interview, this game is a good way of preparing children to speak about even the most unexpected subject. The idea is to take it in turns to think of a truly bizarre question, and then think together about all the different possible ways of answering it.

Accept everything – from the safe and simple to the wildly wacky. Then get your children to choose which were the best ideas and see if they can combine them to form the perfect answer. To get you started, here are a few questions that have apparently been posed by interviewers desperate to find out which of their candidates showed some spark of originality:

- If we define fear as 'something that can hurt us', why are we afraid of spiders?
- If you take one grain at a time away from a mound of sand, when does it cease to be a mound?
- Why don't we just have one ear in the middle of our face?
- If a park has a 'no vehicles' sign, are you breaking the law if you take a pram into it?

Proverbs also offer a good source of ideas. For instance:

- Can two wrongs ever make a right?
- Is a bird in the hand really worth two in the bush?
- When might words speak louder than actions?
- Is all fair in love and war?
- Is it ever worth putting all your eggs in one basket?

CURRENT AFFAIRS

Topical issues offer fantastic opportunities for discussion and developing opinions. Parents often worry that their children don't seem to show any interest in what's going on in the world, but in my experience this really depends on how such topics are presented. If you involve your children in seeking and choosing items for themselves, then there is plenty that they'll find absolutely intriguing. See Chapter 5 for ideas about how to do this.

TED.COM

This website is an absolutely amazing find. It's packed full of video clips of people from all walks of life – scientists, musicians, entrepreneurs, you name it – giving talks about a whole host of intriguing subjects. If you've got older children in their mid- to late teens, you might like to have a family rota where each person takes a turn (say, on a weekly basis) to pick a clip for everyone to watch and then talk about over dinner.

If you go to the 'talks' section, you can select clips by their rating, for example 'most persuasive', 'most jaw-dropping' and 'funniest'. This is a brilliant resource for broadening your children's (and your own!) general knowledge and opening their minds to all sorts of new ideas. It's probably worth a few visits in preparation for university interviews too. When using it, encourage your children not just to accept what they hear. Some of it is controversial stuff: they need to make up their own minds.

Note that this is intended to be a site for adults, and so there's no guarantee that all will be what you might consider 'suitable'! You may want to vet it first ...

JUST A MINUTE

An old favourite – based on the BBC Radio 4 programme with the same name – this game is usually assumed to be more about developing fluency than clearly formed opinions. In fact, it's a great way of introducing all sorts of more complex subjects without your kids even noticing.

A topic is given (which can be anything from cauliflowers to Christianity), and then players take turns to try to speak about it for one minute, with no hesitation (the words 'um' and 'like' are banned), repetition or straying from the subject. Afterwards – and this is where the thinking really comes in – there can be a general chat about which ideas everyone thought were best, which were surprising or controversial and what else could have been included.

DIAMOND THINKING

Another activity that's good for encouraging reasoning and the articulation of opinions, this one can be played anywhere where you've access to a pencil and some sticky notes. There are various different versions, but the basic idea is to generate nine options, which must be ranked in order of importance, in the shape of a diamond. The most important is placed at the top of the diamond, followed by the next two options on line 2, three on line 3, two on line 4 and the least important at the bottom on line 5 (see below).

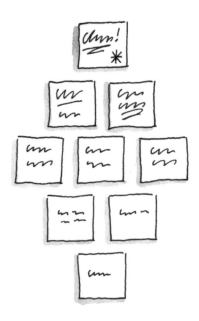

By writing each option on a separate sticky note, your child can keep changing their mind, moving things around and repositioning them until they reach a final verdict. This works surprisingly well in the car, as you can encourage your children to think out loud, telling you what they're doing while they stick their notes on their window. At the end, challenge them to be really persuasive and convince you that their order is the right one.

Try these examples:

- Nine things you could do to improve our garden/street/park.
- Nine secrets of being a good friend/having a happy family/being a successful spy.
- Nine best football players/singers/books/cartoon films.
- Nine colours, in order of happiness.
- Nine objects/pieces of furniture/words you couldn't do without.
- Nine animals/people you'd most like to be for a day.
- If there were nine different professions in a balloon and it was going to crash, how would you decide who should jump out first?
- If we had money to give to protect nine different species of animal, which would you choose?

WHO'S FIBBING NOW?

I couldn't resist throwing this old popular game in at the end – not because it really develops independent thinking, but because it's great for improving fluency and skills of persuasion. Each person selects a really unusual word from the dictionary and then invents three descriptions of its meaning, only one of which is true. The other players have to guess which is the real one.

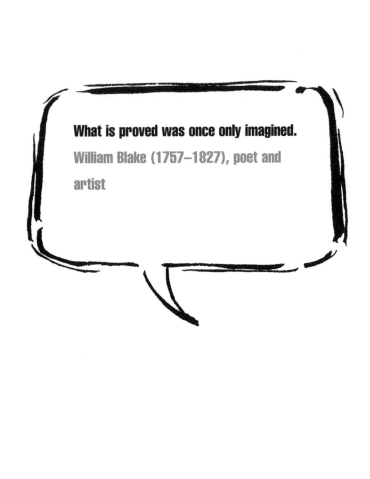

What is proved was once only imagined.

William Blake (1757–1827), poet and artist

2 HOW TO GROW A VIVID IMAGINATION

It's easy to undervalue the importance of imagination. True, pretty much everyone accepts that possessing a rich imagination is a good thing – it transforms children's play, helps them build friendships and creates an inner world that can be a source of great pleasure throughout their childhood. However, we often forget that it's also what underpins originality of thought – the basis for all those creative ideas and solutions that are so valuable in almost every walk of life.

Albert Einstein put it beautifully when he observed that *'imagination is more important than knowledge. For while knowledge defines all we currently know and understand, imagination points to all we might yet discover and create.'*

We tend to assume that all children are naturally imaginative, but it's often surprising how limited this capacity can be (or has become). Maybe because, these days, children have fantasy laid on their laps – or laptops – so there is less need to create their own new worlds and ideas.

Schools certainly help. They do a wonderful job in promoting the development of imagination, in particular in the early years, and this continues in the most part with a focus on learning to write poems and stories. Fewer schools truly make the most of its application in the broader sense, however – being rather tied to the facts and the figures needed for the next exam. And yet imagination is vital to be able to picture a historical scene, to empathise with characters both past and present, and to make the sort of leaps required in understanding more advanced mathematics and science.

To be truly imaginative means to be able to contemplate a reality different from the one in which we live. This is a vital characteristic for anyone who doesn't just want to accept what they're given, who is keen to play a part in improving things – whether it's their lifestyle, occupation or society. Imagination creates the dream. (Later chapters deal more closely with how to go about putting this into practice.)

There are many wonderful things that a parent can do to revive the sense of mystery and magic that can tend to be a casualty of the modern lifestyle. Here are a few ideas to get you started.

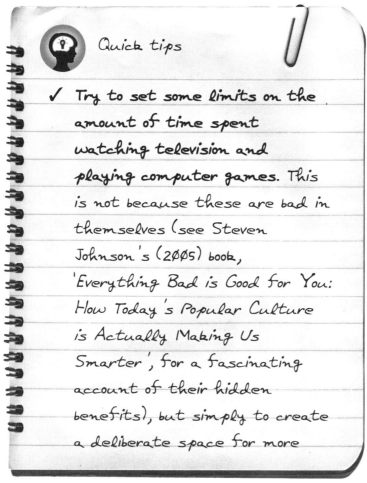

Quick tips

✓ Try to set some limits on the amount of time spent watching television and playing computer games. This is not because these are bad in themselves (see Steven Johnson's (2005) book, 'Everything Bad is Good for You: How Today's Popular Culture is Actually Making Us Smarter', for a fascinating account of their hidden benefits), but simply to create a deliberate space for more imaginative pursuits. Encourage old-fashioned imaginative play by providing plenty of simple props - piles of old cushions and empty cardboard boxes, a sand tray, old tyres and so on.

✓ **Make it a family ritual that you tell stories together.** For example, you could have a 'story dinner' every once in a while - where one person begins telling their own made-up tale, and then everyone takes it in turns to continue the story, each adding a few more sentences. Your stories could be as magical and bizarre as you all wish - the more sensory detail (descriptions of

colours, smells, emotions, etc.)
the better.

✓ **Use story books to stir your
child's imagination.** There are
all sorts of questions that can
be asked that won't trigger
those 'I'm being tested' alarm
bells. Pick questions that
don't have one right answer
but that open delightful,
interesting discussions about
the characters, why they've
behaved as they have, what
might happen next and so on.
This sort of discussion not only
improves your child's
imagination but also can help
them to develop greater
empathy and understanding,

become more perceptive and insightful and even help with their own decision-making and problem-solving. See the activities below for some suggestions.

✓ The great outdoors offers a wealth of opportunities to develop the imagination. A truly inspiring book, packed full of tempting activities, is 'Nature's Playground', by Fiona Danks and Jo Schofield (2005).

✓ Encourage the application of imagination to a wealth of different areas. Try the 'What if...?' game in Chapter 4.

Activities and games

You could try …

THE SQUIGGLE GAME

This is a light-hearted game that's a great place to start when encouraging children to let go of their imaginations. Simply draw an abstract shape or squiggle and take it in turns to say what it could be. When ideas dry up, try asking your child to imagine it from a different viewpoint – as if it's a bird's-eye view from above, as if they're looking up at the object from below, or as if it's coming straight towards them.

HIDDEN TREASURES

If you're the type of person who has developed a collection of weird and wonderful bits and pieces over the years, these can provide a fantastic way of encouraging imaginative and enquiring thought. An old doll wrapped carefully in tissue, a box of assorted beads and buttons, a set of carpentry tools still smelling of sawdust – we forget that these sorts of things can seem wonderfully mysterious to a child. Make the most of this: if you've a bit of free time ahead, bring one of these treasures out with a flourish and a 'Look what I've found!'

Explore the treasures together, with questions such as, 'How do you think this might have worked?', 'Can you imagine what sort of person might have owned this?' and 'I wonder how many different uses we could come up with for this?' Imagine that you could conjure up the genie of the object – a magical person or creature who knew all its secrets. What three questions would you ask?

I know a teacher who, each week, would bring out a different object – perhaps a box or a white glove or a locked diary – and the sense of excitement that was created within that classroom was extraordinary. How did the objects relate to each other? What sort of story is unfolding? This sort of activity doesn't need to be reserved for school – why not try it at home, with a special shelf reserved for mysterious objects? You could involve different people in this: ask friends or other members of the family to bring along something to add when they visit. The objects needn't, of course, be intrinsically valuable – they could be items found outdoors or at the back of those drawers that you rarely open.

Your children might like to create a 'hidden treasures' area of their own – in which case, encourage them to be observant, to keep their eyes peeled for special, 'magical' objects that could be added to the collection. Ask them what each new treasure reveals – are they linked in some form of story or simply special in their own right?

The aim is to encourage children to look at things in a different way – to regain the wonder and magic that sometimes seems to be in danger of slipping away.

MAGIC QUESTIONS

Find time to ask and debate unexpected and magical questions. For instance:

- Imagine you found a secret door hidden in a corner of the garden. Where might it lead?
- If your child's special toy suddenly developed magical powers, what might they be?
- What if you came across the most mysterious house in the world? What would it look like?

This could lead to some wonderful creative activities involving drawing, making things or acting.

EVERYDAY MYSTERIES

I still remember the excitement that my friends and I felt when, as eight-year-old kids, we spent days one summer trying to come up with an explanation for why a scratch in the shape of a girl's face had suddenly appeared on the slide in our garden. We had all sorts of theories – generally based on our conviction that this was surely a significant discovery that clearly meant that someone, somewhere was communicating with us! This sort of imaginative play is in danger of slipping away and yet the creative impulse that it encourages is of the utmost value.

Encourage your child from an early age to look out for everyday mysteries in the world around them. When you're on a walk together, you could point out unusual things – a conifer with one section of its branches missing, a fenced-off patch of unused land, a patch of flattened grass in the middle of a lawn. Play games together where you both come up with magical and wonderful explanations for these mysteries – trying to outdo each other with ever more extraordinary ideas.

WHAT'S IN A PICTURE?

Paintings, drawings, sculptures, book illustrations, photographs in magazines – all these offer wonderful opportunities to develop the imagination. The problem can tend to be that we are so bombarded with visual images that it's more common to skim their surface lightly rather than delve into the wonders of each one.

For this reason, it's sometimes better to pick out just one image on which to focus – perhaps an interesting photograph in a magazine advert or a painting from a book or catalogue. It can help to enlarge this – this highlights its 'special-ness' – but it's certainly not always necessary and you might equally well simply focus on a picture in the story book that you're reading together.

The secret then is to encourage your child to take a journey with you into that picture. You might start with a tempting invitation such as, 'I've found this picture – I really like it but I don't know why. There's something *magical/strange/unexpected* about it. What do you think?' Share ideas together, then probe more deeply with questions such as:

- What do you think this character/animal is looking at? Is it something outside the picture?
- If this picture were trying to tell you something, what would it be?
- If you could step into this picture, how might it feel? What would you do first?
- If you could talk to any of the characters, what would you say/ask? How might they reply?

How do you think the scene might have looked like half an hour later?

CLOUDS

A favourite game – but one that we often forget to play these days – is how many shapes can you see in the clouds? This is a wonderful activity that can be played while out walking or simply when staring out of the window. Encourage lots of ideas and press your child to develop any that are particularly imaginative. For example, if they saw a whale with a big gaping mouth, you could ask them to tell you what it is called, where it's come from, whether it has any magical friends with it, what it's about to do, etc. All sorts of wonderful stories could result...

ABSTRACT ART

Invite your child to draw a picture to represent an abstract noun – something like happiness, love, loyalty or curiosity. You could keep a set of these words written on slips of paper to be drawn from a special bag. Alternatively, try playing different types of music and ask your child to draw what it represents for him or her. Afterwards, encourage a discussion about their choices and ideas.

Encouraging imagination through reading

STORY QUESTIONS

When you're reading with your child, show an interest in their ideas and opinions by pausing to ask the occasional open-ended question. Don't overdo it – you don't want to interrupt the flow of the story and lose your child's enthusiasm. Instead, try to find key moments in the plot when you might both like to sit back, reflect on recent events and think a bit more deeply about the characters and plot. Remember not to turn this into a test – your child will see straight through you! What you are trying to create is a 'book club'-style discussion – simply for the pleasure of it.

Questions can be quite focused, for example:

- What sort of things might x be thinking now?
- How do you think x might be feeling at the moment? What clues are you using?
- Can you imagine what might happen next?

- What would you do if you were x now?
- What do you think of y? Why? How is y different from x?

Or be more general:

- Which of the characters would you most like to meet?
- If you could step into this book for one day, who would you like to be?
- This book is reminding me of z (another book, previously read) but I'm not sure why. Do you think they're similar in any way?
- What was your favourite part of the book? Why?
- Which was your least favourite part?

IMAGINE IF ...

Another great idea is for you and your child to take it in turns to ask each other 'Imagine if ...' questions while you're reading a story together. For instance:

- Imagine if x didn't do that, and he did ... instead.
- Imagine if y didn't exist.
- Imagine if z wore a red dress instead of a white one.

In each case, what difference would it make to the story? What train of events might it set off? Would the story be spoilt? Might it be even more exciting? By playing with the sequence of events in this way, you're helping your children see themselves as potential authors with the power to construct their own story lines and outcomes.

HOW MANY WAYS ...?

Sometimes it's fun to use a story as the basis for a creative thinking challenge. For instance, how many ways can you and your child think of for Roald Dahl's Matilda to defeat Miss Trunchbull, her horrible headmistress? Or for Harry Potter to get his own back on Draco Malfoy?

Encourage lots of unusual, inventive thoughts, and then together choose your favourite ones. How many different endings for a given story can you both think of? Always join in with these activities – it's much more fun for your child and it demonstrates to them that imagination is something wonderful throughout a person's life.

For the deeper thinker

For a more challenging game to develop deeper thinking about a story, author or type of book, see 'What's always true about ...' on p. 45.

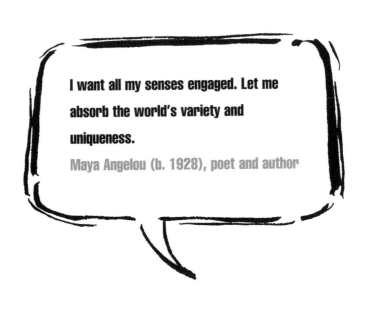

I want all my senses engaged. Let me absorb the world's variety and uniqueness.

Maya Angelou (b. 1928), poet and author

3 HOW TO BE ALERT AND OBSERVANT

We miss so much of what happens around us. It's partly because our lives tend to be so busy that our auto-filter system screens out a large part of what's going on simply to stop our heads exploding! However, noticing things – really learning to keep your eyes open and your ears flapping – is a massively useful skill that for many of us remains underdeveloped. It lies at the heart of understanding, of original thinking – and of humour.

Children are often rather removed from the world around them: unless prompted to do otherwise, they tend mostly to notice things within their own radius. As a result, they can really benefit from being encouraged to develop their senses – from learning to be truly attentive. Whether it's through making the smallest-scale observations in their own back garden or following a series of increasingly complex verbal instructions, if we can help them to develop their capacity to be receptive to what's taking place around them, we're giving them a life skill that will be valuable in all sorts of situations. As the actor Keanu Reeves apparently said, *'The simple act of paying attention can take you a long way'*.

This is partly because if you're the type of person who doesn't need to be told something twice, then it's likely to make you a whole lot more efficient and therefore more respected. But that's not all. It's also the case that we often hear stories of famous people whose success began with a series of fortunate circumstances. Their role was simply to recognise these for what they were and to act upon them, ensuring that they made the most of the opportunities that then arose. Indeed, many of us will – when we look back on our lives – remember occasions of our own when we had no idea that something we read, observed or simply overheard would prove so useful later on.

Life is often unpredictable. It's important that we teach our children to be alert, observant and receptive to the situations it provides.

What's more, encouraging children to make good use of their senses has the added bonus of helping them to develop their ability to concentrate for more extended periods of time. It's also a vital ingredient in building an effective memory.

Of course, it could be argued that this is something that schools already do a huge amount to tackle. However, as many parents know and as teachers will probably be among the first to accept, a lot of children continue to have rather poorly developed listening and observation skills. Some extra help at home could make a real difference.

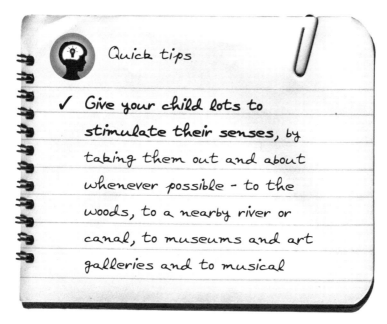

Quick tips

✓ Give your child lots to stimulate their senses, by taking them out and about whenever possible – to the woods, to a nearby river or canal, to museums and art galleries and to musical shows. There are often lots of free events to explore, so keep an eye on local websites and newspapers.

✓ **When you're out with your child, help improve their focus by setting a challenge.** For example, 'Who can find the most unusual thing in the park today?' or 'Who can collect the most things to fit in a matchbox?' Gather collections (with obvious advice beforehand about anything that might be damaging to the health or the environment) and use them to make mobiles or collages or to stimulate stories (see 'Hidden treasures' on p. 27) back home.

✓ If you live in a big town, bus trips are a great way of providing plenty to look at. You and your child could design a questionnaire to take with you, with sections to note the most surprising/beautiful/mysterious thing you see. Sit upstairs and play games to see who spots the most interesting things!

✓ Help your child practise their focused listening skills by encouraging them to repeat, in their own words, what you have just said. Make it more fun by trying this on each other. As your children get older, you could point out that this technique is a really good way of showing that you're interested in what someone is saying and in training yourself to 'tune in' and concentrate.

Activities and games

You could try ...

FIVE THINGS YOU SPOT ABOUT ...

This quick but very effective activity helps develop your child's inclination to watch out for the surprising and the novel and can be used in any spare moments. One player chooses a focus – it could be, for example, a car, a person, a picture, a flower or a building. The other's task is to spot five things about the chosen object that they might not have noticed immediately. This is surprisingly difficult at first and really encourages close observation skills. The first player could then select from the five things the one that they thought was the most interesting or that showed the best powers of super-observation.

This is a lovely activity to play in the garden or the park to encourage a sense of wonder at the abundance and beauty of nature. However, it can equally be used to direct a child's attention to the social diversity and myriad of man-made achievements of the city, to the hidden mysteries within paintings and sculptures, or to the range of expressions, emotions and characters that we see in the people around us.

MEMORY PICTURES

This game can be used with one or more small groups of children, so it can be fun to try when friends are over. It's usually most successful to do this with two or three teams of not more than four children in each.

Find a suitable picture – a cartoon or line drawing of the type found in colouring-in books works best or, if you're about to go on holiday or to visit somewhere like a museum or zoo, a simple map of the area can be an interesting focus. Enlarge it so it's nice and clear, and keep it hidden from the players. Give each group a large sheet of plain paper to share and pencils and rubbers.

Number each child in the group(s), so that they know who is number 1, who is number 2 and so on. Call all the number 1s up at the same time. Give them 20 seconds to look at the picture and then send them back to their team to draw what they remember. After a few moments, call up the numbers 2s for their turn then send them back to help with the drawing. Continue until each person has been up to see the picture twice. After a couple of rounds, it's a good idea to pause and discuss tactics. Have any of the teams discovered any clever tricks for working together?

Before the final round, encourage the teams to take a few moments to formulate a plan of action. Each person will see the picture only one more time. Can they come up with any strategies to make sure they each make the most of their final viewing? Collect in the pictures and award prizes for those that are closest to the original.

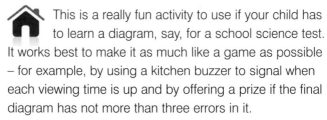

School link

This is a really fun activity to use if your child has to learn a diagram, say, for a school science test. It works best to make it as much like a game as possible – for example, by using a kitchen buzzer to signal when each viewing time is up and by offering a prize if the final diagram has not more than three errors in it.

If the test is particularly important, you could repeat the game two or tree times – once at the beginning of the revision period, once in the middle and once the night before the test. Reduce the number and length of viewings each time to increase the challenge and get your child to spot the differences between their picture and the original each time.

SPOT THE DIFFERENCE

Children love playing this old favourite and it works well as a party game. Depending on numbers, between one and three people stand up in front of the others and a few minutes are allowed for everyone to look closely at them. The people standing up then leave the room and each makes one alteration to their appearance, such as pulling down a sock or swapping shoes. When they re-enter the room, the first person to guess one of the differences correctly changes place with the person whose difference they spotted.

Many variations are possible. If you're playing the game with only one child, you could take it in turns to challenge each other to notice the small changes you have made to a display on a shelf or to the layout of a room.

WHAT'S ALWAYS TRUE ABOUT . . .?

Moving on from simple observation, this activity encourages skills of comparison and analysis as well. The best way to introduce it is in a natural context when you're engaged in something else, such as when reading a bedtime story, feeding the cat or out on a walk. The secret is to sound genuinely ponderous, when asking 'I wonder what's *always* true about . . .?' For example, 'What's always true about fairy tales?', 'What's always true about pets?', 'What's always true about trees?' Then take it in turns to try to come up with answers.

Encourage your child by praising any particularly interesting observations and by pretending to need some 'thinking time' to come up with some of your own answers. Push through beyond the first more obvious answers and see if you can both come up with some more unusual observations.

For the deeper thinker

This activity is great for children who enjoy more complex challenges and it encourages some really perceptive and original thinking. When reading a story, for example, you could ask what is always true about a particular character or about that author. A lovely way to develop an interest in art is to show your child several pictures by a particular artist and ask what's always true about that artist's work.

Remember to point out that you're both basing your answers on limited evidence: your child might like to go away and see if he or she can find an exception to any of the 'rules' you've come up with together, for example by finding a fairy tale that doesn't have a villain, or a painting by the artist that is completely different from the ones you've explored together.

THIS AND THAT

This activity is best carried out when you're engaged in doing something practical with your child, such as making a cake, walking around a supermarket or doing some gardening. The trick is to make it seem less like learning and more of an incidental activity. Pick out two objects that you're using, for example two of the ingredients from the recipe or two items in the shopping trolley. How many similarities can your child find between them? How many differences? As is often the case, you can make this more fun by joining in yourself – perhaps by taking it in turns to generate ideas and making it a game to see who runs out of ideas first.

By the way, a great way to grab your child's attention is to choose two objects that are deliberately tempting, such as two chocolate bars or two types of crisps. This provides a motivating context and children learn a lot from behaving like scientists and carrying out a careful analysis of the items. They could take the activity a step further by grouping their ideas into categories, such as wrapper design, taste, colour, smell, ingredients, origin, manufacturer, etc.

Finish by asking whether, on balance, the objects were more similar than different – or vice versa. It's worth helping children to recognise that their final decision may not always depend simply on the number of ideas on each side but also on their relative importance. For example, two types of citrus fruit may have all sorts of differences, but the fact that they are both from the same food group might outweigh these.

Activities like this will always have most impact if your child can see how they relate to their day-to-day life, so see whether you can both think of other situations where two or more things have to be compared carefully.

School link

 'Compare and contrast' activities often arise at school, but children aren't always shown how to approach these logically and methodically. The answers that arise can be rather waffly and imprecise as a result.

Whether your child has been asked to compare two soft toys, two characters in a book or two proposals to help reduce global warming, the basic skills are the same. Identify and describe the differences and then the similarities – ideally by grouping these into categories in both cases. Then look to see whether the differences outweigh the similarities, or vice versa. Is this what your child expected? If not, why does it surprise them, and (for the older child) could this result have any implications?

MIX 'N' MATCH

This game is popular with children of all ages. It encourages them to use their imagination and think creatively, while also developing their observation skills.

One person should be the 'finder'. Their task is to choose any five objects from around the house/garden/park – wherever you are. The other players take it in turns to sort the objects into two piles, one of two and one of three items, using some form of logical classification method (e.g. colour, size, shape, etc.), which they must keep secret.

You may need to help younger children with this concept at first, as they will often sort objects in ways that are far from logical! If this happens, it can help to ask questions such as:

- Why have you placed these objects in a separate group?
- How does this object fit with the other one/two? What's the same about them?
- Does that reason help us understand how these objects are different from the ones in the other group?

Each time the objects are sorted into two piles, the others try to guess what the method is. You can play for points if you wish – so that a player guessing correctly gains one point – but it works equally well just to praise interesting ideas and thoughtful guesses. When you've run out of ideas, repeat with someone else taking on the role of 'finder'.

For the deeper thinker

This activity can be made more creative by sorting the objects into two random piles. Your child could do this with their eyes closed or by picking the items from a plastic carrier bag. Now their challenge is to work out a way in which the two piles are different. Can they spot any common features between the objects in each pile? If they manage this immediately, see if they can find two more ways of doing this.

READ MY MIND!

Another version of the activity above is to set one person the challenge of finding 15 different objects. These are then spread out where the others can clearly see them and the finder picks one and pretends to think really hard about that object. The others' task is to read their mind and work out which one they have chosen. They can ask up to five questions to help them with their task but these can only be answered yes or no. For instance:

- Is your object made of plastic?
- Is your object just one colour?
- Does your object have any see-through parts?

Young children find this quite difficult at first and tend to waste their questions by asking ones that are too narrow (e.g. 'Is it the toy giraffe?'). It's really interesting to see their observation skills and logical thinking improve.

SORTING PROJECTS

Try to find ways of involving your child in real-life sorting projects. This works best if it looks as though you need your child's help. For example, you might say something like, 'I've just realised it would be really useful to make a list of the pictures that are all around the house so we've got a proper record of them – but I don't know how to sort them into different types. Have you any ideas?' Other options could involve sorting out the contents of a cupboard or drawer or finding a really inventive way to sort all the books on a shelf.

This is a great way to encourage close observation skills and lots of logical thinking. Take it in turns to come up with as many different ways of sorting the things as possible. And don't just stick with the first few more conventional ideas – push on through that quieter patch, taking thinking time to encourage some really off-the-wall ideas.

Once you've lots of ideas to choose from, get your child to pick his or her favourite and to reveal to you the thinking behind this. Then it's time to put the project into practice.

TUNE IN!

Next time you're out and about – whether in the garden, on a train or walking to school – ask your child to join you in trying to count and identify all the sounds that you can both hear. Make it a challenge – can you hear 10 or even 20 sounds? It's interesting for your child to find out how many sounds we blank out most of the time. Which sound is their favourite? Why? Can they focus on listening to that sound only, blocking out all the others, while you count in your head to ten? Can you do the same?

Gradually build up the length of time and see if you can both manage to block out other thoughts during this listening exercise. It's harder than it sounds.

MYSTERY SOUNDS

This popular game helps encourage listening skills. Give each player a bag and get them to spend a little while on their own, secretly 'gathering sounds'. They might, for instance, find a wooden spoon and a saucepan, or a beanbag that can be shaken. Once the collecting time is up, players meet back and take it in turns to sit behind a chair and make each of their sounds. The others guess how the sounds are made – and whoever is right gets a point.

And another thought!

This activity works really well with smells and tastes as well – though needs more supervision for the sake of safety!

BLIND MAN'S JOURNEY

Following the same theme as the previous activity, this game develops your child's listening ability while also helping to improve their communication skills. The object of the game is for the speaker to guide the blindfolded listener from the beginning to the end of a trail in as short a time as possible. To make this trickier, the trail should be set up by a third person and should be littered with a variety of obstacles. For example, your route might take you between two chairs, around a table, over a log, through a gate and so on – with a length of rope or hose marking the course.

Safety considerations clearly need to be taken into account! This definitely works best outdoors, where there's less risk of breaking the family heirlooms. It's also a good idea to assign your third person the role of 'watcher' to oversee the process and make sure that no one is about to fall down the stairs or walk into a tree...

Young children find it surprisingly difficult to give clear directions, so begin with a fairly easy trail. After that, the complexity of the course is up to you.

ALL EARS

This is another useful activity to help children develop their listening and concentration skills – and this one's great practice for school too, as classroom situations frequently rely on children correctly remembering a series of verbal instructions.

Draw a simple picture and make up a set of clear instructions for creating an exact copy. For example, your first instruction might be 'Divide your page into two halves, by drawing a line across the middle from left to right', followed by 'In the right-hand half, draw a circle to fill the whole space', and so on.

Give each player a plain piece of paper. Explain the following rules:

- There will be a series of instructions that will be read aloud, sometimes one at a time, then later two or three together.
- They will not be repeated: each instruction will be read only once.
- You must sit on your hands while the instruction is being read.
- When you've heard the instruction, you should do what it said.

At the end, get your child to compare their picture with the original and see how they've got on. What score out of ten would they give themselves? Many young children find this very hard at first, but it's really encouraging for them to see how they improve with practice. They'll love creating a picture of their own to try on you too – and this provides great practice with communication and logical thinking.

School link

This is a good activity to help children learn mathematical words such as 'horizontal' and 'vertical', and two-dimensional shapes such as hexagons and equilateral triangles.

IT'S A WACKY WORLD

A much more imaginative variation on the old 'I went to the supermarket and bought ...', this game is hugely popular and encourages players to develop focused listening skills as well as challenging their memories.

The first player begins with 'In my wacky world ...' and then adds a simple fact, such as 'the sky is green like jade'. The next repeats this, then adds a second description, such as 'In my wacky world, the sky is green like jade and cats own all the supermarkets'. Continue until one player eventually gives up.

For the deeper thinker

If your children want to learn a 'magic trick' to help them remember long lists of information, you could teach them the 'journey method'. An extremely effective memory tool, this requires them to picture a journey, looking out as they do so for the key highlights on the way – particular features like a road sign, traffic lights, a garage and so on.

When trying to learn their list of facts (or, in the case of the game above, of bizarre descriptions), they should picture each one in turn at the different locations on their journey. So, for instance, they see themselves leaving their house, and as they do so, they look up and notice that the sky above their home is bright green. As they reach the post box at the end of their street, they spot a group of cats handing out leaflets about the opening of their new supermarket. You get the idea! It's really fun to try and, because a journey can have almost limitless features, it's a brilliant way of remembering a huge amount of information.

TOUCH IT!

This activity is designed to stimulate a younger child's sense of touch and to improve their language skills. Each player should gather a set of perhaps three to five different objects or substances that they think the other players will find difficult to identify by touch alone. Then take it in turns to be blindfolded and to focus on one item at a time, describing it carefully before making any guesses.

This is a simple game, but great fun – and children enjoy trying to find objects that they think might fool you. When it's your turn to make a guess, model the practice of feeling each object very carefully – using a range of descriptive words each time.

THE MEMORY WALK

Help your children to develop a heightened awareness of their senses and much more effective memory skills by encouraging them to revisit special events with you. Pretend you're taking a memory walk together – back to a particular visit or occasion that you both enjoyed. Describe it together, as if you were wandering around the scene, pausing to stop and notice the sounds, sights and smells along the way.

Ask each other questions to prompt further memories. Can you smell anything particular at this point? What do you notice over there above the . . .? How is so-and-so looking? Your children might find it helpful to keep their eyes closed during this activity.

This is an amazingly strong exercise. If repeated, you (and your children) will find you remember more and more each time. It also means that special occasions – and even those day-to-day events that otherwise slip out of our minds so quickly – are more likely to find a permanent place in your memory.

School link

If your child has taken part in a school trip or there has been a special event such as an author visit or sports match, encourage them to take you on a memory walk with them, describing it all as clearly as they can so that you can really imagine you were there. This will have the added benefit of helping your child enormously when it comes to creative or report-writing, as they will immediately have a much wider collection of sense-memories to draw upon. It's also invaluable practice in articulating their thoughts.

Millions saw the apple fall, but Newton was the one who asked why.

Bernard Baruch (1870–1965), financier, statesman and presidential advisor

4 HOW TO KINDLE A BURNING CURIOSITY!

Evolution has programmed children to be inquisitive, to seek explanations and to do their best to make sense of this extraordinary world. Sadly, growing up too often dampens this enquiring spirit. To paraphrase the education and culture critic Neil Postman, children enter school as question marks and leave as full stops.

This is partly our fault – both as teachers and as parents. Children see adults answering questions far more often than asking them. They come to assume that asking questions is something you're meant to grow out of: it's a sign of immaturity, of weakness. Answers – knowledge – are what count.

And yet the ability and inclination to probe, to explore, and to know how to ask perceptive, challenging and open-ended questions is something of enormous value. Samuel Johnson (1709–1784), author, editor and moralist, famously noted that *'curiosity is one of the most permanent and certain characteristics of a vigorous mind'*. It signals an active, open, problem-solving spirit and, as such, not only lies at the heart of successful learning and research but also is the key to creativity, innovation and progress.

The speaker and entrepreneur Anthony Robbins, said: *'Quality questions create a quality life. Successful people ask better questions, and as a result, they get better answers.'*

We need to do everything we can to keep children's curiosity alive. Fortunately, asking 'thinking questions' is a skill that can be practised, just like any other skill – and it's amazing how quickly you'll see the changes that result. Young children in particular are still at that wonderfully curious stage and they respond really well to being challenged to think of ever more interesting, unusual and 'out-there' questions.

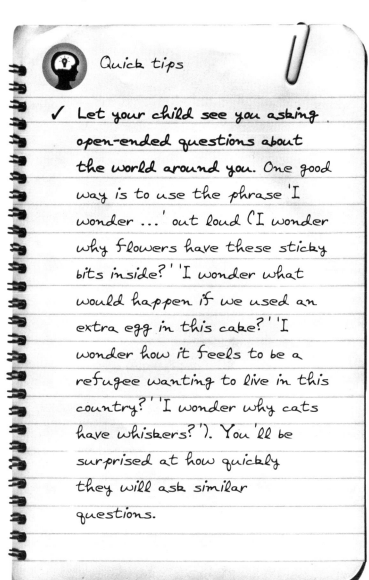

Quick tips

✓ Let your child see you asking open-ended questions about the world around you. One good way is to use the phrase 'I wonder ...' out loud ('I wonder why flowers have these sticky bits inside?' 'I wonder what would happen if we used an extra egg in this cake?' 'I wonder how it feels to be a refugee wanting to live in this country?' 'I wonder why cats have whiskers?'). You'll be surprised at how quickly they will ask similar questions.

✓ Switch the focus from praising your child for their right answers to praising them when they ask really interesting or unusual questions. Don't be afraid to admit it when you can't answer their questions. Instant answers are rarely the best ones anyway. Instead, celebrate the fact that your child has asked one of those questions that (a) has always bothered you but to which you've never found a suitable answer; or (b) has never occurred to you.

One way of responding is by saying something like, 'That's a really interesting question/idea/suggestion. I'm going to need some thinking time for that one' or 'What a great question – I'm really impressed you thought of it. I'd like to think about it and get back to you when we've a bit more time – is that OK?' This shows your child that you don't have all the answers and that that's fine. It also teaches them to take 'thinking time' too.

✓ If your child asks a particularly interesting open-ended question, it could be a good chance to put your heads together and come up with a few possible theories. Keep this activity playful and exploratory – perhaps by taking it in turns to come up with ideas. Avoid leaping in with the right answer – remember, you're encouraging your child to do the thinking.

Activities and games

You could try ...

THE 'WHAT IF ...?' GAME

Take it in turns to come up with as many 'What if ...?' questions as you can. These could be linked to the situation you're in – for example, how many 'What if ...?' questions can you think of that relate to things you see on the way to school? Or while at the supermarket or during a visit to the zoo? Alternatively, they could be inspired by a book your child is reading, or by a broad area such as science, nature, space or numbers. Sometimes they might just be completely zany and open-ended.

Here are a few examples:

What if animals learnt to talk?

What if everyone had an identical twin?

What if human beings had three legs?

What if no one ever told the truth?

What if the temperature increased by 5°C over the next 100 years?

What if people lived to 200?

Children love this and, when encouraged, they learn to come up with some really imaginative questions. When a really good one pops up, stop and dwell on some of their ideas for possible consequences. (When I recently asked a group of kids the question 'What if human beings had three legs?', they came up with ideas I'd never have thought of –

from 'It would make driving easier as you've a foot for each pedal' to the slightly more disturbing 'You could use your extra leg to trip people over'! The great thing is that there's no 'getting it wrong' – so it's a non-threatening game that really encourages curiosity and creativity.

MAKE A WONDER WALK

Create a template with several 'thought clouds', each containing the words 'I wonder ....'. Cut these out and share them between the members of your family. Encourage everyone to 'think big'! What do they wonder about? You could mention that this was how great thinkers in the past made new discoveries – by asking 'I wonder how that works?', 'I wonder why that happens?' or 'I wonder what would happen if . . .?'

Get everyone to jot down one question in each bubble, together with an illustration if they wish. Create a trail of questions around the house or garden and explore the questions together – picking out the ones you're each most interested in investigating or discussing further. (This activity is adapted from an idea in Guy Claxton's book, *Building Learning Power*.)

QUESTION STARTERS

Children find it much easier to learn to ask interesting and unusual questions when they're given some 'question starters' to get them going. Make a poster together to go on the wall, listing several possible ways to begin a thinking question.

A great way to get everyone involved is to have a notice board that displays your family's questions on sticky notes – perhaps with a different colour for each member of the family. This immediately shows your child how important it is to ask questions and how this continues right through life – it's not something you're meant to 'grow out of'. Questions can be jotted down whenever someone thinks of one and then used as prompts for discussions at mealtimes or in the car.

FINGER QUESTIONS

This is a good one for the car: one person picks an object, place or person. The players then take it in turns to ask five questions about this object, using the words 'why', 'when', 'how', 'where' and 'who'. Young children find it harder than you'd think, but you'll be amazed at how much more interesting their questions will become with a little prompting and praise.

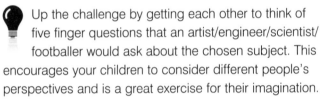

For the deeper thinker

Up the challenge by getting each other to think of five finger questions that an artist/engineer/scientist/footballer would ask about the chosen subject. This encourages your children to consider different people's perspectives and is a great exercise for their imagination.

MAGIC POWDER

Imagine that someone famous is coming to tea! It might, for instance, be a current celebrity or a person in the news, a character from a book or film or a particular historical figure. Invite your children to pretend that they have some magic powder that they're going to sprinkle over their visitor. It will grant them the power to ask any five questions they wish – and the response will be the whole truth and nothing but the truth! What will they ask?

THE FAIRY QUESTION-MOTHER

Rather like the previous activity, this game requires your children to imagine that someone is going to pay them a visit – but this time it's their fairy question-mother. She will be able to grant them the answers to any three questions they would like to ask. Start thinking! What will they choose?

KEEPING A QUESTION LOG

Another lovely idea is to help your child make his or her own 'question log' – a special booklet for special questions. These can be recorded as and when they arise, and then used as a prompt for discussions.

School link

 Encouraging children to come up with questions that they are genuinely interested in is a great way of getting them to take a more active interest in topics at school. What does your child wonder about his or her current history or geography topic? What magic questions would he or she choose to ask a relevant historical figure, a famous composer or a particular scientist?

A list of their top five questions could be made to take to school. Most teachers will be delighted to see their pupils getting involved in this way and, I hope, will find time to discuss the questions or to guide your child with some research.

Try to learn something about everything and everything about something.

Thomas Henry Huxley (1825–1895), biologist

5 HOW TO DEVELOP A 'LET'S FIND OUT' APPROACH

As I said earlier, children learn all sorts of things at school. Mostly though, it's stuff they've been told they *have to* learn. The best schools and teachers will at least try to create opportunities for their pupils to ask and investigate their own questions within a given topic, but this is still relatively rare, and restricted by the need to cover certain areas within a specified amount of time. And yet the world is such a fascinating place. Surely one of the most valuable things our children can grow up with is a deep curiosity, followed by the desire to try to unravel the mysteries it holds.

This is especially true given the ephemeral nature of knowledge. There are, of course, certain things that it's vital everyone learns. But for the vast majority of the time what we learn at school in terms of actual subject content is ultimately of little use to us. Think back to your own childhood. How much of what you learned proved valuable later in life? More tellingly, how much can you even remember now?!

To paraphrase the psychologist B. F. Skinner, *'Education is what is left over when you've forgotten everything you were taught'*. Some forward-thinking schools are taking this on board by beginning to teach something called 'learning to learn' – and this is a really valuable move forward. It's all about creating transferable questioning, research and information-processing skills that will apply in a future where change is really the only certainty. After all, we've no idea what knowledge will be of most use in the future – and it's extremely likely that most of the truly valuable stuff hasn't yet been discovered, let alone packaged up for schools. What our children really need to develop is the capacity to learn whatever they need to learn for the situations in which they find themselves – and to be able to do so with enthusiasm and confidence.

W. Edwards Deming, an American statistician and business advisor, put it rather neatly: *'Learning is not compulsory. Neither is survival.'*

As well as being prepared for change, being an effective 'finder-outer' acts as a safeguard in all sorts of situations. Your children will be less likely to be duped (the rogue tradesperson comes to mind, but these days it could equally well be the private equity investment advisor) and more likely to be able to make decisions based on a careful comparison of their options.

Alongside this, it is important that our children grow up with an urge to find out more about the wider world in which they live. Increased globalisation means that, to be successful, people will need an understanding of the inter-connectedness of events and the impact of issues on us all. This makes them better equipped to form opinions about the bigger picture and puts them in a stronger position to make a real difference to the world. And in the shorter term, it's also going to impress the school or university interviewer who sees a dozen clueless candidates for every one who actually knows what's going on in the world.

There's a great deal of scope at home for encouraging children's interests in a broader sense. Some children will just naturally seem to be on the look-out for things to investi-gate, often with their own quite strong ideas about what they do and don't find interesting. However, others may need a bit more encouragement – especially as they get older and are increasingly influenced by an education system that subjects them to particular topics rather than allows them the chance to explore.

The previous chapter contained lots of ideas that could be used to spark interesting investigations. Here are a few more strategies to use that can help children develop the independence to see these through.

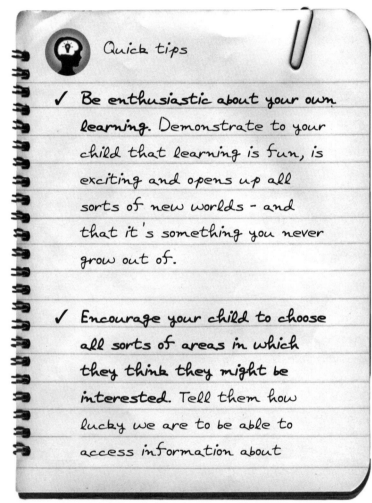

Quick tips

✓ Be enthusiastic about your own learning. Demonstrate to your child that learning is fun, is exciting and opens up all sorts of new worlds – and that it's something you never grow out of.

✓ Encourage your child to choose all sorts of areas in which they think they might be interested. Tell them how lucky we are to be able to access information about virtually anything we want – from the migratory habits of penguins to the mechanics of an Aston Martin DBS V12 (James Bond's car of choice). There's so much to discover. Remember that, at this stage, you're hoping to help them become confident and enthusiastic learners, so it really doesn't matter what they choose to investigate (within certain legal and moral limits, of course!).

✓ Facilitate this by taking your child to the library. Support them in using Internet search engines for their research and perhaps provide them with a

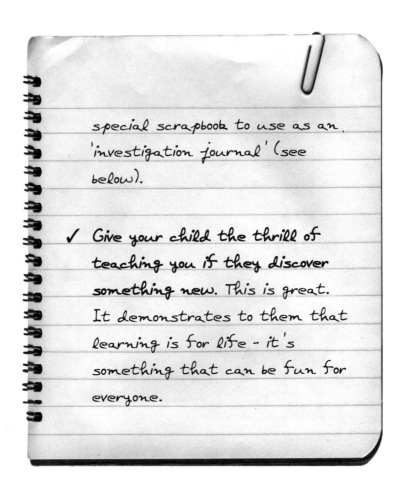

special scrapbook to use as an
'investigation journal' (see
below).

✓ Give your child the thrill of
teaching you if they discover
something new. This is great.
It demonstrates to them that
learning is for life - it's
something that can be fun for
everyone.

Activities and games

You could try ...

BE A DETECTIVE!

Introduce, from as early an age as possible, the idea that we are all 'learning detectives' when it comes to finding out about the world in which we live. Encourage your child to follow the steps below.

1 **Select the investigation.** What would you like to find out about? Have you thought of an interesting question that you'd really like to answer?

2 **Consider where to search.** Where might be a good place to look for relevant information? The computer? An encyclopaedia? The library? A particular person?

3 **Search for clues.** Gather information, take notes and carry out interviews. Pursue in more depth any particularly interesting leads that arise during the investigation.

4 **Make some deductions.** What do *you* think of what you've found? Have you come up with any thoughts or ideas of your own?

5 **Compile a report.** What are the three most important things you've discovered?

You could make a 'detective' poster together, with five footsteps on it, each big enough to use to record the stages of the investigation.

INVESTIGATION JOURNAL

Give your child a special notebook for their investigations, ideally with both plain and lined pages, and set aside some time together to create a suitable cover. It could, for example, be a collage of fragments of newspapers or photocopied excerpts from books about topics that your child finds interesting. Alternatively, it might be covered with different pictures of famous fictional sleuths and symbols.

Inside the front cover, your child might like to include a

poster of the type described above. Keep the next page blank for a list of contents that can gradually grow, perhaps entitled something like 'My record of investigations'. Then help your child pick their first question to explore.

Findings can be recorded in whatever way most suits your child – and they certainly don't need to be written out in neat paragraphs. For instance, pages can be divided up into boxes, with one interesting fact or idea in a different colour in each. Or the investigation question could be recorded in the middle of a page, with all your child's ideas and pictures around it – either randomly noted or arranged roughly into areas in a mind-map form. One page could be set aside for 'Top ten most interesting discoveries' and another might contain 'My favourite websites', with a brief summary of each. See the next activity for further ideas.

FUN WAYS TO RECORD STUFF

There are all sorts of ways of noting down interesting information, which children will find infinitely more tempting than simply writing it out in sentences.

Probably the most well-known of the visual methods, Tony Buzan's Mind Maps® have been used successfully within education and business all around the world. The main benefit is that the process of creating a Mind Map obliges the person to organise what they know rather than to simply copy it out. Your child should begin with their paper in landscape format and then write the title of their topic in the centre. Next, they decide on how many sub-topics it can be divided into and give each one a different-coloured branch. At the end of the branch, the sub-topic should be divided further into key points. See *Mind Maps for Kids: An Introduction* (Buzan, 2003) for examples.

An alternative is to make a mandala. This time, the title of the topic is written in a circle in the middle of a large sheet of paper. Another circle is drawn around it and then divided into three or four main sub-topics, using a different colour for each. Further circles can be added, each time dividing the topics further until all the relevant details are also recorded.

A simpler option is to create a tree diagram, with the name of the topic at the top of a page and a series of sub-headings written on the next level down. Your child can then list all the things they discover – important facts, words, etc. – under each heading. A different colour could be used for each section of the tree diagram to make the final result more eye-catching and memorable.

There are all sorts of other ways of displaying information. Your child might like to take a topic and turn their notes into a poster or diagram, with labels to explain the different areas. If they're artistic, they could convert it into a cartoon strip with speech bubbles to explain what's going on in each picture. Sets of little fact cards can be made, with a 'Did you know …?' fact and picture on each one. These are particularly popular, as your children can use them to impress their friends and family!

School link

 It's still too often the case that children are told simply to 'go home and revise' when the dreaded exam time comes around. And yet everyone is different – and to become an effective learner involves finding specific study strategies that suit you, your personality and your way of working.

Even if you only ever manage to get your children to try the sorts of methods described above very occasionally, you're giving them a massive advantage in a totally different way, as they're also very effective revision techniques. However, they are all examples of 'visual' methods. If you're interested in investigating more practical strategies – ideas that might appeal to the type of child who likes talking and doing more than looking and reading – have a look at the parents' version of the *Revision Passport* (also by the author), available at **www.learn4life.co.uk**

THE DETECTIVE'S TRAIL

This one's more labour-intensive and so is likely to be less suitable for busy families. However, it's worth remembering as an activity to try during the summer holidays if you're running out of ideas for home entertainment.

Encourage your child to pick an investigation, and then help them to draw up a simple record sheet. Let's say, for instance, you have a daughter who wants to find out more about underwater animals. Start by taking it in turns with her to come up with lots of interesting questions to explore, such as 'How many different types of dolphin are there?', 'What does an octopus eat?' and 'What are the weirdest methods that underwater creatures use to ward off enemies?' Jot down each of these and then get your daughter to pick her six favourites.

Divide a page in the investigation journal into six different sections and give each question its own space. Now gather a variety of sources (books, computer, newspapers, etc.) and place them in different locations around the home. (If you've time, it will be even more tempting for your child if you leave a secret hint at each one, directing them to their next spot – but that may well be going too far for most parents who are already rushed off their feet.)

Follow the trail together – or get your child to try this with a friend and offer a prize if they answer all the questions. At each source, skim the evidence for clues that might help answer any of the questions and record these in the appropriate section of the sheet. Some children might like to use a different-coloured pen for each question: this sort of visual clue can be helpful later when organising and remembering the information.

What did your child discover? Did they find out anything surprising? If they could remember one thing for the rest of their lives, what would they choose? Why? If they've done this activity with a friend, can they pretend to be top experts and act out a short documentary to teach you about what they've discovered?

School link

 This trail technique is a really good method to use for research-based homework. It makes the task much less daunting and somehow much more fun – especially for more active children who find it hard to sit still.

NEWSFLASH!

Research doesn't always need to focus on facts – personal opinions and memories can be equally important in some areas. If your child has chosen the sort of question where opinions matter, then encourage them to create a reporter's interview sheet in their journal and to pick a few people who might have something to say on the matter. They might, for instance, interview a neighbour, a sibling, a relative or a teacher. The answers that your child gathers could be turned into a short newsflash item, which could be taped and played back afterwards.

For the deeper thinker

This technique can be good for approaching those 'big questions' that more able children sometimes desperately want to discuss. 'What happens to my pet when it dies?' 'Is there life on other planets?' 'Why do some people lose everything in floods?' In these cases, it's worth briefing the interviewees beforehand . . .

GADGETS GALORE

Whenever something breaks – an old hairdryer or radio, for instance – don't just throw it away. Keep it for future investigations – either in the garden on a sunny day or as a great way to spend a rainy afternoon. Your child will love taking things apart – and you can turn this into a game by setting mini-challenges, such as 'What's the oddest component you can find?', 'How many other uses can we come up with for this bit?' and, later, 'Can you put it all back together again?!'

SECRET SCIENCE

A great way for your child to develop a questioning, investigative nature is by dreaming up and carrying out their own secret experiments. For instance:

- What impact does a smile have?
- What sort of boat can I make that will travel the furthest down the stream?
- How does our pet mouse/dog/cat spend an average hour?

Whenever an idea occurs to them, they could jot it down in their investigation journal – to be followed up one day when they're at a loose end.

If you've time, help your child to consider what sort of information they need to gather, how they will collect the data and how they will record their findings. They might like to give a presentation to the family when the final results are known.

EXTENDED INVESTIGATIONS

By using these sorts of methods, you are playing an extremely important role. Because somewhere along the line, your child may discover a real passion – and whether it's for astronomy or gardening or car maintenance, it really doesn't matter. To have a burning fascination for something is a wonderful thing – it gives us determination and drive, keeps us alert and active, and develops our research skills, persistence and an attention to detail. These sorts of qualities and skills are invaluable later in life, and so early practice is really useful.

I know of a teenage girl who is passionate about American politics, and her knowledge and enthusiasm are deeply impressive. She stands out from the crowd when you're talking to her – because that sort of drive and enthusiasm is sadly so rare today when we give so little time to helping the young identify their passions. Her passion is now driving her ambition – it's given her a chance to find a unique reason for believing in herself and her place in the world.

Once a genuine interest has been identified, do all that you can to help it blossom. You could, for instance, set your child a challenge: a keen botanist could be given a patch of garden to transform; if you have a potential astronomer, get them to produce a *Duffer Parents' Guide to the Stars*;

your budding actor could be given the responsibility for producing and performing a play for your friends and neighbours. Such projects will of course need to be adapted to suit children of different ages – and ideally, of course, your child should be involved in choosing for him- or herself something that seems really exciting.

The final step is to try to show an interest without taking over – always a tricky balance. Ideally, you want your child to feel supported, while also in charge of the overall direction of their project. See Chapter 16 for more ideas.

Encouraging an interest in current affairs

This is a potentially delicate but extremely important area: on the one hand, adults sometimes grumble that kids show no interest in the world around them; on the other, we hear that the children of today are increasingly stressed about the big issues that fill our newspapers – global warming, war, terrorism and the like.

The problem is, if 'the news' is ignored – at home and at school – then children tend to pick up only on the negative headlines, which serve both to turn them still further from developing a genuine interest in current affairs and to fill them with an uncertain horror about the future. We have an important part to play in helping our children to develop a balanced perspective and in opening their eyes to the extraordinary and fascinating spectrum of facts, issues and stories that surround us.

PICKING A SUITABLE PAPER

Remember that your child is young. He or she is unlikely to get wildly excited by issues from the *Financial Times*, even if this is the stuff that makes your own world go round. By subscribing to newspapers that are more child-friendly as well as the ones you normally read – or picking up the occasional lighter-weight evening paper – you will immediately find that the sort of issues raised will be of more appeal to your child.

If the thought of this fills you with horror, bear in mind that you're playing a long-term game here. Your aim in the first instance is to help your child discover that newspapers are both accessible and fascinating. If this means you have to – for a while – buy a paper that has a reading level of an eight-year-old, then so be it. It will pay off in the long run.

And another thought!

 There are some great websites and services that are now provided for parents and schools, as a means of making the news more accessible to young people. Some examples are:

FirstNews – an award-winning weekly newspaper for children aged 7–14, explaining the stories behind the week's main headlines (**www.firstnews.co.uk**).

Newsademic – an online newspaper designed for the younger reader (aged 9–16). This contains clear outlines of major stories, together with definitions of key terms (**www.newsademic.com**).

CBBC – the BBC provides an excellent online source of news items and activities for children (**http://news.bbc.co.uk/cbbcnews**).

WHAT'S IN THE NEWS?

Have a news board somewhere in your home where different members of the family can pin up interesting headlines and short articles that catch their attention. To introduce this, ask your child to help you make the board, decorating it with a suitable border and giving it a headline such as 'What's going on in the world?' or 'Would you believe it?'.

Keep the selection changing regularly – and try to pick stories that are really eye-catching. Younger children often love stories about animals, celebrities, outer space and sport – so these are the sorts of things to go for initially.

As children get older, it's extraordinary how many topical issues are of potential fascination to them. As a teacher, I have seen children debate with real interest and passion issues such as global warming, animal rights, smoking bans in public places, freedom of speech, the threat of terrorism, human cloning, euthanasia, renewable energy sources … the list is endless.

WHAT'S MISSING?

On your news board, your children could set challenges for each other and for you by cutting out headlines that catch their attention and blanking out a key word or short phrase. This one's fun to think about over a meal – with bonus marks for anyone who comes up with either the right answer or just a really silly alternative!

NEWS SCRAPS

If it looks as though your child is showing an interest in, say, animal research, then keep your eyes peeled for articles or letters that have something interesting to say about the subject.

Your child might like to keep a scrapbook or use a section of their investigations journal, with different areas for different topics that they've found surprising or intriguing.

NEWS TIME

Teach your child that newspapers are like secret chests – with the occasional golden nugget lurking inside waiting to be found. Your child will be delighted to discover that reading a newspaper is not like reading a book – very few people start at the beginning and work through to the end. Instead, it's all about skimming and scanning and picking out the bits that catch your eye and appeal to your own particular interests.

You could set aside a 'news time', when you and your child each curl up with a newspaper and take it in turns to tell each other about a particular story that has caught your interest. Keep these descriptions short and snappy – just enough to give the other person an intriguing glimpse of the story. Remember that you are trying to demonstrate that your own paper holds stories of interest to a child as well. Avoid using this as a chance to go into lengthy detail about the latest stock-market collapse or the history of Zimbabwe. Children will come to these sorts of issues in their own time. In the meantime, try to match the type of story your child selects and be patient – the level will gradually change with age and maturity.

For the deeper thinker

This activity can be extended by setting a further challenge: can you and your child summarise your chosen articles in no more than 20 words? It's quite tricky and takes some clever use of words, but it really helps the reader get to grips with the essence of the story.

TOPICAL TALKS

In the first chapter, I suggested having a weekly discussion time – perhaps over dinner or during a regular car journey. Your child could pick a topic from the news board described on p. 87 and take it in turns with you to come up with questions that could be asked about that particular topic. Then pick the question that might be most interesting to pursue.

The main thing to remember is that your purpose is to spark your child's interest in events that are going on in the world around them. You may be able to drop in a little background information and knowledge if you feel that this is really important, but that shouldn't be your main objective. Instead, ask your child what he or she thinks. Keep this fairly short and use open questions that don't have one 'right' answer. For instance:

- What do you think is interesting/funny/surprising about the topic? What is worrying?
- If you had magic powers, is there anything you would do or change?
- Can you think of anyone who might have a different opinion about this?
- If you could ask the know-it-all-wizard-of-the-world one question about this topic and get a truthful answer, what would the question be?

By all means, add in your own opinion occasionally – but only ever as another possible viewpoint, and never in a way that puts down the ideas your child has suggested.

Remember one of the first 'top tips' of this book – offer specific praise. Comment on any ideas that your child comes up with that are particularly pertinent or any observations they've made that show they have really thought about the issue. They will glow with pride if you are able to show them that you take their opinions and ideas seriously.

NEWSROUND

If this is all starting to sound rather too heavy, remember that it really does all depend on how it's presented. One way of introducing a lighter-hearted element is to get your child to pretend to be a news reader and present a quick two-minute news summary to the rest of the family. He or she could pick out a few stories, then sit at a news desk and present short summaries of these to the audience.

If you have a larger family, your child might like to interview different people, asking them for their thoughts about a particular story. Make this really exciting and official by filming it and starting with the words, 'Lights, cameras, action!'

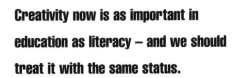

Creativity now is as important in education as literacy – and we should treat it with the same status.

Sir Ken Robinson (b. 1950), creativity expert, author and government advisor

6 HOW TO ENCOURAGE ORIGINALITY AND CREATIVITY

Creativity is not only about the arts. It's about ideas – ideas that may sometimes be turned into extraordinary paintings, poems and plays, but that equally could result in scientific breakthroughs, ingenious new products, improved methods and procedures, innovative management styles, ground-breaking policies and laws, previously undiscovered solutions to complex problems ... Progress, basically.

The economist John Maynard Keynes put it beautifully when he said, *'Ideas shape the course of history'.*

And it's never been more true than today. In such a fast-paced and erratic world, creativity is a vital ingredient if we – and our children – are to make the most of the opportunities, dilemmas and mysteries that are continually thrown at us.

The problem is that we tend to be better at judging other people's ideas than actually having them ourselves. This is partly because our education system rarely places much emphasis on the generation of new ideas – if you want a good grade, it's much safer to repeat what your teachers have said than to take a risk and come up with something more original. As creativity expert Roger von Oech (1998) explained, *'Much of our educational system is an elaborate game of "guess what the teacher is thinking". Many of us have been taught that the best ideas are in someone else's head.'*

Unfortunately, it's precisely this sort of experience that probably helps to confirm our suspicion that some people are just born more creative than others – and, too often, that we're firmly in the 'not creative' camp! However, while there are almost certainly some naturally creative geniuses out there, it's also true that very many of us have allowed obstacles to get in the way that prevent us from realising our creative potential.

There are certain beliefs and habits, which – if ingrained from an early age – can dramatically increase the confidence and creative ability of your child. This chapter focuses on laying these foundations. See also Chapters 7 and 14 for further practical applications of this essential mindset.

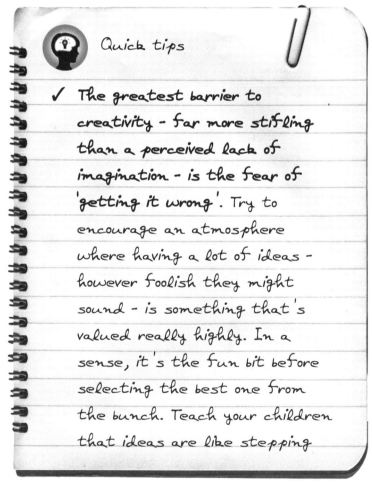

Quick tips

✓ The greatest barrier to creativity - far more stifling than a perceived lack of imagination - is the fear of 'getting it wrong'. Try to encourage an atmosphere where having a lot of ideas - however foolish they might sound - is something that's valued really highly. In a sense, it's the fun bit before selecting the best one from the bunch. Teach your children that ideas are like stepping stones – even the most ridiculous ones might lead to something brilliant later on. They'll love this, because it's sadly rare for them to find themselves in a situation where nothing they can say is too silly.

✓ **Don't be afraid of laughing at each other's ideas.** Remember that you are trying to develop robust, confident children who can see the funny side of their own and other people's ideas, while at the same time being able and willing to scrutinise even the most unexpected suggestion in case it prompts something new or useful.

✓ **Create plenty of opportunities for growing originality.** Asking questions that fit with whatever you're doing is a great way to start – though be careful how you do this. If you're out on a walk and you lob an unexpected 'Why do trees have bark?' at your child, they're going to feel like they're at school. Simply rephrasing this as 'Look at the bark on this tree. It's amazing, isn't it? I wonder how many theories we could come up with for why trees have bark?' transforms the activity into a far more tempting game that you can both share. It could be a take-it-in-turns competition to see who runs out first or a shared goal of reaching 20 ideas together.

✓ **Pretend sometimes that you don't have any more ideas.** Say something like 'OK, now - I'm not going to panic - give me a few thinking moments' before coming up with your next suggestion. This will help your child to learn that the best ideas sometimes take time and effort.

Activities and games

You could try …

CREATIVITY MOTTOS

There are some absolutely wonderful quotes about creativity that can become really valuable mottos that children quickly learn by heart. Four great ones are:

> 'If people never did silly things, nothing intelligent would ever happen' – *Wittgenstein, philosopher*.

> 'The best way to get a good idea is to get a lot of ideas' – *Linus Pauling, Nobel Prize-winning chemist*.

> 'Ideas are like rabbits. You get a couple and learn how to handle them, and pretty soon you have a dozen' – *John Steinbeck, author*.

> 'It is better to fail in originality than to succeed in imitation' – *Herman Melville, author*.

Make posters together with your child to display and illustrate their favourite quotes.

ALTERNATIVE USES

Why use a cheese grater simply to grate cheese? It could also be a model for a skyscraper, a new type of bird-feeder or a musical instrument. Choose a random object – for example, a corkscrew, paper clip, cotton reel or coat hanger (or try one of the objects suggested by Malcolm Gladwell, 2008, for his preferred test of intelligence – a brick or a blanket) – and have fun with your child thinking of alternative uses for it.

Think about the object's properties – its shape, what it's made of and so on – as this can help to prompt some really original ideas. Persist beyond the obvious first few ideas: how could it be useful in a hospital, in a supermarket or underwater? What could an elderly person, a teenager or an air steward use it for? With a little help, children often surprise themselves with how many ideas they can generate.

A practical and fun extension of this activity is to give your child something really commonplace, such as a box, a piece of kitchen foil or a sheet of newspaper, and see how many different things they can think of making with it.

RUBBISH!

A variation on the activity above, this game works best with two players. The first person begins, 'In the rubbish bin, I found ...' and finishes the sentence with an object of some sort that might feasibly be thrown away, such as a rotting kipper or a broken toaster.

The second player has to respond, as quickly as possible, with 'which could be used to/as a/for ...' to describe some novel way of recycling that object. The toaster, for instance, could be dismantled and used to create a sculpture; the kipper could be attached to a post in the garden to ward off burglars ...

The players then swap roles and the game is repeated. This game is great fun and inspires all sorts of innovative ideas. It works best if the pace is kept reasonably fast.

20 WAYS ...

This is a lovely game to play whenever there's a spare moment. Who can think of 20 ways to ... make a tree happy, remove a bull from a china shop, teach a chimpanzee to play football? The sillier, the better!

SOMEONE ELSE'S SHOES

Sometimes new and more imaginative ideas emerge when we deliberately view a situation from another person's perspective. This game introduces this trick. Tell your child you've got a secret challenge in your head and get them to choose any person they want, for example a friend, a teacher, a famous footballer, a pop star, a member of the royal family – it's up to them. Then set the challenge. For instance:

- What would *x* do if he/she ruled the world?
- What would your school be like if *x* was in charge?
- How would *x* raise money for charity/improve our local park/redesign the bathroom?

CONNECT – DISCONNECT!

This is a great game for car journeys where there are several passengers willing to play. The rules are simple: take it in turns to call out a word that is connected in some way with the word that the previous person has said. So, for instance, the first word might be 'blue', the next 'sky', the following one 'clouds' and so on. A player is out if they (a) say a word that connects to an earlier word by mistake, (b) answer too slowly, or (c) repeat a word that's already been said.

Repeat the game, this time with the new rule that the word must *not* be connected in any logical way to the previous one. This is harder than it sounds! Other players can call 'Challenge!' if they spot a link between the two words – though they must do this before the next person has said their word.

WHAT WAS THE QUESTION?

The answer is ... gold/glass/it was like a dream. What was the question?

Surprisingly tricky, this one – especially if you add the extra challenge that the question must be one that leads only to that particular answer.

NAUGHTY WORDS

This is a game for three or more people. One person chooses a word, which might be an object, action or concept, and whispers it to the next person, together with three strongly linked 'naughty words'. The second person's task is to describe this word to the other players without using these key words. For example:

- Pizza [naughty words: cheese, Italy, round]
- Happy [naughty words: smile, feeling, laugh]
- Jogging [naughty words: running, fit, healthy]

CRAZY CONNECTIONS

What connects an elephant and a teapot? Or a picnic and the crown jewels? Children love this game and it's a great way of improving lateral thinking skills. Simply place lots of random words in a bag and take it in turns to pull out two at a time. The challenge is to find as many crazy connections as possible.

Another variation that works really well is to use action phrases, such as 'washing the car', 'jumping on a trampoline' or 'whistling a tune'. This introduces the concept of analogies: how is riding a bicycle like doing a jigsaw? As always, everyone should keep thinking beyond the obvious answers, as the most inventive ideas usually take time to form. Afterwards, you could ask whether, on balance, they thought it was a strong or a weak analogy.

In both cases, it works best to get children involved in thinking up the words or phrases themselves – they can write them on slips of paper themselves or, if they're younger, you may prefer to act as scribe.

CONCEPT COLLAGES

This one's good for rainy afternoons, as it is very absorbing and takes a bit more time. It's basically a brainstorming technique and can be used to encourage children to explore their own thinking about a range of topics. You will need a large sheet of paper, some coloured pens or pencils and some old magazines.

Help your child to pick a subject. A good one to start with is 'imagination', but it works equally well with anything your child is currently interested in – a particular hobby, for example, a favourite football team or a book they are reading. In the centre of the paper, they should write their title. The task then is to fill every space of the page with ideas, words and pictures that are linked with that topic.

One interesting way of structuring this is to use a different-coloured pen or pencil to indicate each particular level of exploration. Taking the 'imagination' topic as an example, your child could pick a colour and draw arrows from this central word out to five or six other words that come into their head when they think of 'imagination' (such as 'stories', 'brain', 'new worlds', 'daydreaming' and 'magic'). Next, they switch to a different colour to follow up each of these words, drawing more arrows out from each word to new linked ideas. This helps them to organise their ideas and to remember to pursue each train of thought.

You and your child will both be amazed at the number of ideas that are thrown up in this way. These can be written in words, illustrated as pictures or represented by photographs and phrases cut from old magazines. The end result is frequently fascinating, but it's the discussion along the way that really opens your eyes to how your child thinks.

For the deeper thinker

This works well as a means of unpicking abstract concepts, such as emotions (anger, love, courage), characteristics (beauty, curiosity, friendship), subjects (history, art, science) and words linked with current affairs (environment, war/peace).

School link

Concept collages offer a fun and creative way of delving into a huge variety of school topics – from science subjects such as electricity, to historical characters such as Florence Nightingale, and cross-curricular topics such as transport. They have the advantage of not really seeming like work, while encouraging your child to think surprisingly deeply about the subject – which in turn can give a clear insight into what they do and don't understand.

LOONY LOGIC

For this game, simply think of a proposition that no one would ever consider and set each other the challenge to persuade someone as convincingly as possible that it's a good idea! This is great for developing communication skills and quick lateral thinking, as you need to turn off your normal 'logical mode' and look at the situation from a completely different angle. For example, how would you persuade someone that:

- all shops should be built underground?
- by law everyone should wear purple?
- there shouldn't be any seats in trains?
- every household should own a giraffe?
- books should be banned?
- no one should ever be allowed to look in a mirror?

Set a time limit of, say, one minute, to make this more challenging for older children.

FLOG IT!

As with the game above, this requires a lot of lateral thinking, this time to be able to identify the unique selling points for some very unlikely products. Players take turns to set each other seemingly impossible challenges, such as 'Can you sell a ... bottle of fresh air? A box of mown grass? Yesterday's toe-nail clippings?' (The yuk factor really come into its own with this game!)

Their opponent has to come up with as persuasive a sales pitch as possible. When children are younger, it's likely that they'll simply give examples of what the product could be used for, but older ones will enjoy using the sort of language they hear in adverts on television. When they run out of ideas, they switch over and set a challenge for the next person. Children love this (don't bother awarding points – just keep it light and funny) and the creativity that results can be pretty impressive.

I AM LIKE A . . .

This is a very easy game to try when there are a few spare minutes. Take turns to ask each other a question of the following type and see what sort of answers result: 'What animal/colour/musical instrument/item of clothing/type of food is like you? Why?'

Note that this is very different from asking what type of animal/colour/food you like. This distinction sometimes needs to be made.

CREATIVE CHALLENGES

Don't underestimate the value of getting together with your child and simply making stuff. The challenge could be to create a home for one of your child's toys, a play-thing for the family pet or a wacky sculpture for the garden.

If possible, keep a big box of goodies stashed away somewhere – old boxes, fabric, cardboard tubes, cotton reels, bits of string, all those components from ancient gadgets that never quite made it back into a reassembled state (see 'Gadgets galore' on p. 82). You name it – it's probably got some potential for a new incarnation.

Designers, engineers look at the same things as everyone else. But they see something different. And they think what it could be – and make it happen . . .

James Dyson (b. 1947), engineer and inventor

7 HOW TO BECOME INNOVATIVE AND INVENTIVE

You may well be thinking that teaching your eight-year-old how to be an inventor is pretty low on your list of priorities. But I'm including this chapter for a very good reason. Having led countless lessons, courses and competitions designed to get kids thinking about what the next must-have gadget might be, I've discovered – quite simply – that they are better at it than we are.

And it gives them a real kick to find this out. How exciting to discover that new inventions aren't created in mysterious laboratories by people in white coats but are simply the product of some serious creative thinking on the part of someone (or a team of somebodies) just like them. It may well be that they don't decide to go on to become the next James Dyson or Anita Roddick – but, when you think about it, new products and applications are an important part of the development of virtually any organisation. We need inventive people in all walks of life. They're extremely valuable and, as such, are very much sought after.

It's also the case that developing an entrepreneurial spirit and an 'I can make a difference' mindset can really boost your child's confidence and self-belief. You're teaching your child that the world is not something that needs to be accepted just as it is, that situations are malleable and products changeable and that they have exactly the right skills and character to make a real difference to people's lives.

As John Schaar, professor and political theorist, said, '*The future is not just some place we are going but one we are creating*'.

In *The Sunday Times* book about entrepreneurs, (called *My Big Idea*), Emma Harrison, founder of A4e, a training and employment organisation, says: *'the best ideas are the simplest ideas. They are the ones that come from people using a product or service which is inadequate and deciding they can do better ... You can't just sit in your room in isolation and come up with an idea. You have to be out there travelling, talking, reading, watching, listening, experiencing. It is then that you will spot something that you don't like and decide to do it better'* (Bridge, 2006).

The suggestions below lead on from earlier activities to develop the imagination, the inclination to be observant and the confidence to generate ideas. They are very practical and a lot of fun. Your children will love them – and you never know, one of their ideas might just work ...

Quick tips

✓ Encourage your child to notice the design of everyday things. Why do they think a teapot/fridge/radio is the shape it is? What's good about the design? Why do so many houses look just the same? Is there a reason for it?

✓ Linked to this, teach your child to question the status quo. After all, the way we've been doing things for years isn't always the best way. Ask 'How could we do this differently?' and 'Might there be a better way of designing that?' and look out for simple ways of putting this into practice. For example, when driving home from school, your challenge together could be to find different routes each time – perhaps the one that is most beautiful, the quickest or the one that uses the least petrol.

✓ Point out to your child that although market research is a good thing and it's worth considering other views very carefully, they shouldn't be put off if people don't immediately believe in their ideas. Tell them stories about how some of the most successful products were initially greeted with scepticism. Henry Warner, president of Warner Brothers, apparently asked, back in 1927, 'Who the hell wants to hear actors talk?' and Ken Olson, founder of Digital Equipment Corporation (later bought by Compaq), declared in 1977 that 'There is no reason why anyone would want a computer in their own home'.

✓ **Teach your children that occasionally the best ideas come out of the blue.** Sometimes, after being immersed in the intricacies and practicalities of a problem, the answer arrives in that unexpected 'Eureka!' moment – when you thought you'd switched off and your attention was elsewhere. For a fascinating discussion about this, try Guy Claxton's (1997) book, 'Hare Brain, Tortoise Mind: Why Intelligence Increases When You Think Less'.

Activities and games

You could try ...

GO SHOP!

A walk around a department store is a fantastic way to stimulate an inventive mind. Set a challenge of some sort – or, better still, get your child to think of a really interesting challenge for both of you. For instance:

- What are the five most bizarre/useful/ridiculous items that you can find?
- If you could be the inventor of one item in the shop, what would you be most proud of? Why?
- Can you find three things you never knew had been invented? What score out of ten would you give them?

Let your child take a digital camera along to record their discoveries. That way, on the journey home, they can be narrowing down their final list to present to you.

IMPROVE IT

Choose an everyday object – something we tend to take entirely for granted, like a coat hanger or a television or even an elastic band. Consider its features first of all – what is it made of? How does it feel? What colour and shape is it? What functions does it have? Then think about its limitations – what's wrong with it?

When I play this with a class, we stand in a circle and the

children pass the object around, taking it in turns to point out what it can't do. Ideas can be as sensible or silly as the children want: 'The problem with this elastic band is ... that it smells horrible', ' ... that it pulls your hair when you have a pony tail', or ' ... that it can't fit around an elephant' (which, of course, begs the question 'When might it be useful to put an elastic band around an elephant?', and you have your next creative thinking challenge!).

This sparks all sorts of ideas for the next round – where the children come up with suggestions for how to improve its design. They might suggest covering the elastic band with a soft, slippery material, for example, or creating a range of bands that smell of different fruity flavours.

Point out that this is how new inventions are born – simply by people who don't accept the status quo. You'll be able to think of all sorts of examples of this – for example, fitted sheets, the Swiss Army knife, spreadable butter, mobile phones with Internet access, wheelie bin covers, spectacles with television screens inside them ... Encourage your child to look out for these too.

Ideally, as with many of the games in this book, it works well to integrate this activity into the normal routines of everyday life. For instance, if you're brushing your child's hair, you could both chat about the hairbrush – does it really have to be the way it is? What might the 'next generation' of hairbrushes be like?

An alternative is to set your kids a specific challenge one rainy afternoon, such as to invent the next flavour of crisps or design a brand new videogame. Get them to draw and label a picture of it. If they get really involved, they might like to plan and perform an advert for their product too. This links well with the activity 'Advert alert' on p. 194 as you can tell your children that they need to know the tricks of the trade if they're going to try to create their own persuasive pitch.

WACKY INVENTIONS

It's really fun to investigate the sort of ideas that are already being developed. Encourage your child to be an invention-spy and use the Internet to uncover the latest weird and wacky ideas. This works best if you pick a product on which to focus, for example a toaster or a mobile phone. Simply type in 'wacky toasters' in the images function of your search engine and you'll find all sorts of incredible ideas – from see-through toasters to toasters that fry eggs, play the waltz and print your chosen picture on the bread!

Your child might like to design a poster or keep a scrapbook as an ongoing project, with different pages devoted to different products. Note that this one may need to be supervised, unless you've got filters set up to allow your children to browse the Internet safely on their own.

ONE IDEA SPARKS ANOTHER . . .

Another great way of encouraging inventiveness is to take an existing object and think about how its design could spark an idea for a completely new product. Consider the features of the item, and then ask whether it could be adapted in some way or put to an alternative use. Could its size or shape be changed? Could it be made out of a different type of material? Could a special feature be added?

Two of the many wonderful ideas for inventions that have come out of my classes illustrate how this process can work:

- **Butterstick**. Olivia Maneeroj, aged 10 at the time, chose a glue stick as her inspiration. Instead of glue, however, she planned to fill the tube with a chilled stick of butter (which, she decided, would be sold in packs of refills). This could be wound out and spread on to toast without the wastage and washing up involved when using a knife.

- **Vanish varnish**. Khushali Halai and Jenna Noronha, both aged 11, teamed up to adapt a normal ink pen and turn it into a very handy gadget for your pencil case or make-up bag. Their idea was to fill the pen with nail varnish remover instead of ink, and then to add a disposable nib at one end and a detachable wipe at the other (both of which would be sold separately in packs). So much more practical than the old-fashioned bottle of liquid and endless balls of cotton wool!

Children love inventing. With a little direction, they are absolute naturals at it – not having the sense of limitation and practicality that so often prevents us from giving it any thought. You might even consider holding a neighbourhood 'Dragons' Den' event, where your children and their friends pretend to be on the television show and pitch their ideas to a panel of adults.

MAKING UP NEW GAMES

This is a really fun activity for a sunny afternoon in the garden or park – but one that can work equally well indoors so long as you hide anything precious! Give your child a small selection of objects – about five or six would be plenty; for example, a skipping rope, a plastic jug, a bar of soap, an (old) empty picture frame and a golf ball. The challenge is to invent a game that makes use of each of these items.

Dreaming up the rules of a game is both a creative activity and an exercise in logical, sequential thought (though your child may not realise it). If children are working in a small group, then it becomes even more interesting, as a significant degree of collaboration is required for the activity to work. It's a great opportunity to reinforce one of the secrets of creativity – that the best ideas build upon rather than conflict with each other (see Chapter 15).

Of course, the game then needs a name and the activity can be extended in all sorts of ways – such as holding a mini-tournament, designing a box for the objects with a set of rules, or even creating a television advertisement for it.

INTO THE FUTURE

Peering into the future provides a perfect opportunity for focusing your child's inventive spirit. What might homes look like in 50 or 100 years' time? Would there be entirely different rooms? Might they be made of different material? How might environmental issues affect future design?

Similarly, your child might like to consider future forms of furniture, transport, entertainment or communication. The list is pretty much endless. They might be inspired to create a whole book of futuristic designs ...

For the deeper thinker

Introduce your child to the drawings of Leonardo da Vinci – the ultimate example of someone who dreamt up all sorts of futuristic designs, some of which have since sparked real inventions.

IMAGINE THAT ...

Sometimes it's from considering hypothetical situations – both the plausible and the silly – that new ideas and inventions are born.

Imagine, for instance, that you had to invent a practical device for animals that would save the biggest chain of pet shops from bankruptcy. What would it be? Or imagine that you had to invent something that would make life easier for blind people – or something that could help a teacher create just the right atmosphere for his or her class. Imagine that people lived forever. What inventions might be needed?

These are the sorts of questions that you can have great fun debating with your child. Get a really big sheet of paper spread out on the table and start doodling.

And another thought!

 More 'Imagine that ...' activities can be found in the set of *Just Suppose ...* and *Just Suppose ... Too* cards (also by the author), available at **www.learn4life.co.uk**

IMPROVE IT: SITUATIONS

Apply this spirit of invention to situations as well as to items. Ask your child to consider, for instance, what could be done to improve the local park or town centre, or to make your supermarket more user-friendly. They might even like to write to their local MP with their ideas. The point is to empower them: to teach them that their ideas matter, and that even if they can't make a difference immediately, they can start to practise.

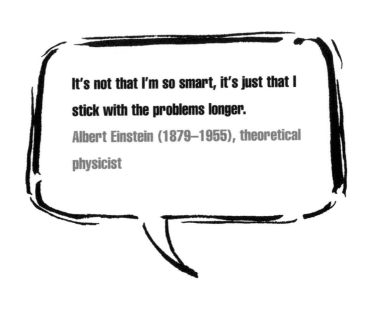

It's not that I'm so smart, it's just that I stick with the problems longer.

Albert Einstein (1879–1955), theoretical physicist

8 HOW TO DISCOVER THE MAGIC OF PERSISTENCE

Robert Half, author and recruitment consultant, said that *'Persistence is what makes the impossible possible, the possible likely, and the likely definite'*. In other words, it really is magic stuff.

In fact, of all the characteristics researched for this book, this is the one that seems to be quoted by the most people as being highly significant in driving their own success. Having an inner desire, a fighting spirit, a real determination to achieve whatever it is that one sets out to achieve – this is a secret ingredient that truly sets certain people apart from others.

When you think about it more closely, it's really three qualities rolled into one: first, the ability to stay focused, to avoid distractions and to see something through; second, a willingness to struggle when things are hard – to keep trying and, if necessary, to come up with different approaches when solutions and answers aren't immediately obvious; and finally, a personal striving to be the best that one can be – an unwillingness to settle for the slapdash or the 'good enough'.

The problem is – as many parents and teachers will contest – some children just seem to have a persevering nature, whereas others don't!

It may be that there is something inherent in each of us that determines our natural persistence level. However, it's also likely to be affected by two other key factors:

- Do we have a clear reason for persisting?
- Have we learned how to make persisting pleasurable – or, at least, less painful?

It's just the same for our children. Many children are unlikely to learn to persevere unless they're taught explicitly why and how to do so. It's rarely the easiest course of action, especially when the sun is shining or there's something good on television. And yet nearly every child has the capacity to persist beyond what we would ever imagine – as is demonstrated by the commitment they're often willing to give to the latest computer game. Many are willing to spend hours in pursuit of that elusive 'next level' – coping with repeated failure along the way by simply telling themselves that next time they might succeed. If we could only bottle this ...

Well, perhaps to an extent we can. This chapter offers a few suggestions.

Quick tips

✓ Show your child that persevering is not easy for anyone. Share your own thoughts with them, for example, by saying: 'Oh, I'm finding this really hard. But I'm going to stick with it because I know it will make Grandad really happy/help pay for our next holiday/be worth it in the long run etc.

✓ From an early age, talk about 'persistence muscles' (Claxton, 2002). Help your child to understand that learning to do anything new is bound to hurt at first. This is absolutely natural – and is the case for virtually everyone. What matters is what a person does with this hurt. Do they panic and give up or do they take a deep breath, try again and stick with it until their 'muscles' are built up a bit more and it seems easier?

✓ Teach your child to recognise and control those negative thoughts that so often persuade us that we're not good enough, that we won't be able to do achieve what we want to achieve. Pretty much everyone hears that glum inner voice sometimes – your child could give it a name and picture it as a real character whose sneaky mission is to try to get them to give up! It's really important that we fill our children with confidence in themselves. A positive attitude – not blindly optimistic, but believing in the power of persistence – will make an enormous difference.

✓ Praise your children for their effort and persistence rather than for their intelligence or for absolute levels of achievement. Research has shown that this is much more likely to motivate children who might otherwise avoid more challenging, interesting tasks for fear of failing and losing your admiration. What's more, children who receive praise for their hard work and persistence tend to blame any failure not on a lack of ability but on not trying hard enough. This keeps them positive and means they're more likely to put in the effort next time.

✓ Be firm when your child has started an activity and wants to give up part-way through. This is natural - it's far easier to begin lots of things than to finish one. Your role is to help your child learn that the pride and satisfaction gained from seeing something through to a successful conclusion usually makes 'sticking with it' worthwhile. (Of course, there may be exceptions where it makes sense to give something up as a bad job. However, this is very different from simply abandoning an effort because of a short attention span.)

Activities and games

You could try ...

PERSISTENCE POSTERS

The first question to tackle is: why persist? Fortunately, there are hundreds of fantastic quotes about the importance of persistence – something that surely goes to show just how valuable this particular trait is.

Why not choose three or four of your favourite quotes and make them into posters to display around the house? Or, better still, tell your children that you've found these wonderful quotes that you really love and you wonder if they'd mind picking a few and using the computer to make them into posters for you. Seeing posters like this on an everyday basis means that the persistence message is much more likely to sink into their subconscious and to become part of the way they think – especially if seen from a very early age.

As with almost everything in this book, you're likely to make more of an impact on your kids if you present these ideas as discoveries that you're making for yourself – things that you think might be really important for you. They'll be much more likely to want to join in if they don't think you're trying to teach them something!

---

15 Great Persistence Quotes

"Genius is 1% inspiration and 99% perspiration" - Thomas Edison

"By perseverance the snail reached the ark" - Charles H. Spurgeon

"I hated every minute of training, but I said, 'Don't quit. Suffer now and live the rest of your life like a champion'" - Muhammad Ali

"If people knew how hard I worked to achieve my mastery, it wouldn't seem so wonderful at all" - Michelangelo

Most of the important things in the world have been accomplished by people who have kept on trying when there seemed to be no hope at all" - Dale Carnegie

"Let me tell you the secret that has led me to my goal. My strength lies solely in my tenacity" - Louis Pasteur

"Failure is usually the line of least persistence" - Wilfred Beaver

"Age wrinkles the body. Quitting wrinkles the soul" - Douglas MacArthur

"Big shots are only little shots who keep shooting" - Christopher Morely

"It does not matter how slowly you go, so long as you do not stop" - Confucius

"Perseverance is the hard work you do after you get tired of doing the hard work you already did" - Newt Gingrich

"The man who can drive himself further once the effort gets painful is the man who will win" - Roger Bannister

You don't win an Olympic gold medal with a few weeks of intensive training" - Seth Godin

"Talent is cheaper than table salt. What separates the talented individual from the successful one is a lot of hard work" - Stephen King

"When I thought I couldn't go on, I forced myself to keep going. My success is based on persistence, not luck" - Estée Lauder

ROOM FOR PERSISTENCE

Many children find it hard to persevere with homework. Rattling through it and producing something that 'will do' is often the preferred option. For this reason, it's the perfect testing ground for developing good persistence habits.

It sounds bizarrely obvious, but you can really help your child learn to focus by making sure they have a suitable place to work. This may be a comfortable chair with a well-lit desk at an appropriate height – probably away from the noise of television, radio and siblings – but it may even sometimes be a beanbag or a high stool in the kitchen. Children, like adults, vary and there are no hard and fast rules about when, how and where to work. You could even turn this into an investigation with your child – where he or she tries out different positions and places over the course of a week or two, noting on a scale each time how much it helped or hindered their persistence.

If you have a child with a particularly scientific bent, this could be turned into a 'fair test' – a concept that most will understand from school. They might, for instance, decide to investigate the impact of background noise – doing their homework on Monday, for example, with the radio playing, on Tuesday with some pop music, on Wednesday with classical music, on Thursday with the TV on, and so on. After each session, your child could keep a record of how they got on – perhaps by making a few written notes in an investigation diary and giving their concentration and progress marks out of five.

Another week could be spent researching the best time for homework. Your child could try doing their work immediately on getting home, after a short break and light snack, after watching television, after dinner, etc. As before, the purpose is to find out what works best for them. And by doing so, they are learning to create the best conditions to help them persist.

MAGIC EYE PICTURES

A lovely practical illustration of the magic of persistence, these pictures can be found in books and on several Internet sites. An easy way to find them is to type 'magic eye pictures' into the images section of a search engine.

On first sight, they look like random patterns and colours. On second sight, it's just the same! In fact, it takes most people absolutely ages to see what's really there. The trick is to hold the picture right up to your nose, so that it's totally blurry, then move it gradually away from your face. Keep your eyes slightly out of focus. When it works (which it will do, finally), you'll see a three-dimensional image 'magically' leaping out of the picture at you.

CONCENTRATE!

This is a good game – if you can bear it – for kids to play on long car journeys, as it directs what is often their natural inclination to wind each other up!

One person sets the other a challenge. It could be to sing a well-known nursery rhyme or pop song or to give a one-minute talk on a particular topic. The first person, meanwhile, will do everything they can (without touching the other person or raising their voice too much) to distract them. They could sing or make funny faces or make some sort of repetitive noise or movement. If the other achieves their challenge without pausing, they get a point.

ON THE BRIGHT SIDE ...

It's important that we teach children that persistence does not *replace* thinking. It doesn't mean sticking blindly with something, regardless of the outcome. As Einstein once said, 'The definition of insanity is doing the same thing over and over again and expecting different results'. True persistence requires creativity – a willingness to keep coming up with new ideas until you find your best one.

For this game, three players are needed. The first person offers a starter sentence that describes a seemingly bad event (which could be something fairly mundane or completely silly – both work well). For example:

- Oh no! I forgot my best friend's birthday ...
- Oh no! I've broken my pencil ...
- Oh no! I've just fallen off a cliff ...

The other two players then take it in turns to reply by looking on the bright side. For instance, the third example above could be finished with 'Yes, but on the bright side ... you get to find out if your super strength hair gel works' or 'Yes, but on the bright side ... you'll be first to the beach'. The first player times them, allowing up to 20 seconds for each idea.

This develops both creative thinking and persistence, as the players should keep coming up with ideas until one of them fails to do so within the 20-second time limit. It's worth listening in on this game occasionally: sometimes you'll be staggered at your children's ingenuity. You can also usefully point out that some of their best ideas are those that come later, when they've kept thinking beyond the normal 'give-up' point.

CONSTRUCTION AND BALANCING GAMES

There are some wonderful construction kits on the market that are brilliant for encouraging patience and persistence. *Marble Maze* by Lagoon Games, for instance, is a simple but fantastic wooden kit made up of different shaped blocks and tubes. It takes a surprising amount of creativity and logical thought to build a structure through which the marble will run without getting stuck, but, when it works, the satisfaction that kids of all ages gain from this is immense. It's a bit extravagant, but if you can lay your hands on two sets, then the opportunities to create really innovative structures are far greater.

Another is *Penguin Pile-Up* by Ravensburger, where children take turns to balance a colony of penguins on a wobbly iceberg. Great fun, and persistence is definitely the name of the game.

PERSISTENCE PAYS

Why not consider occasionally linking your child's pocket money to some form of perseverance challenge? Let's say that you'd like them to learn to build up a level of persistence with keeping their room tidy or practising a musical instrument. You could use a 'Who wants to be a millionaire?' approach: if they achieve the target on Monday, they've clocked up 20 pence, on Tuesday it goes up to 40 pence, on Wednesday it's 80 pence and so on (obviously you can adjust the amounts). If they don't persist one day (unless they've a seriously good excuse), it could drop back to zero!

A PASSION FOR PERSISTENCE

The fact that kids are so happy to persist for endless hours with their computer games suggests that part of the problem is that the sort of things at which we want our children to persist are often not things they'd choose for themselves. Their reluctance is entirely understandable – few of us would be willing to devote time to something for which we can see little point or personal benefit. This means we've got two options:

- **Help them to recognise the longer- (and shorter-) term benefits of persistence.** Children need to be helped to look ahead and to see a real reason for sticking with something. And the more precise, the better. Simply suggesting that it will lead to a 'better future' won't tend to work with most kids. Try to find something that your child will value to act as a goal. (See Chapter 16 for more ideas about this.)

  Sometimes, however, the longer-term benefits are just too far away to help. Persistence for endless stretches of time (or even, in a child's world, for a whole hour) can seem far from appealing. This is especially true when it comes to revision. Even a child who has a healthy internal drive to succeed may find it difficult to get past the short-term tedium of revision when they'd rather be shopping or playing with a friend.

In these cases, help your child to discover that persisting doesn't have to be 'all pain and no gain'. Teach your child to plan and control their own short-term rewards as an incentive for persisting. Get them to make a list of suitable treats – like watching a particular television programme, having a chocolate bar, phoning a friend, reading a chapter of a book or playing football for ten minutes. These can then be used to break their work into emotionally manageable units – with the prospect of something fun ahead acting as a good incentive to keep going. By taking charge of this themselves, your children are developing a really valuable skill that will help them throughout their life.

Help them to find something they can feel truly passionate about. As mentioned in Chapter 5, it's worth helping your child discover something they can feel truly motivated by. Whether it's collecting comic books or breeding spiders, the point is that having a passion can teach a person a great deal about the magic of persistence.

The added bonus is that you can use this as a fantastic way of encouraging them at other times, along the lines of 'Remember how brilliantly you did … when you stuck with it night after night for a fortnight!' True, applying it to the latest bit of geography homework may be less of a draw, but it should help them to begin to see the link between persistence and success.

PERSISTENCE ROLE MODELS

There are lots of great persistence role models for your children – sports stars, actors, scientists, singers, even politicians.

It's worth researching a few of these and mentioning them every now and then. Not as a lecture – but perhaps as something you just read about that struck you as really amazing. You don't need to end it with 'and that's why you should persist with your homework'. The message will sink in gradually on its own.

Here are a few ideas to get you started.

The scientist: Thomas Edison (1847–1931), American inventor

As a young boy, Thomas Edison was pulled out of school after teachers called him 'stupid' and 'unteachable' (Zeleznock, 2008). He was fired from various jobs, but he never gave up his real passion – inventing. During his life, he obtained 1093 patents for new inventions – many of which were unsuccessful. Some, though, were ground-breaking – such as the electric lightbulb, the gramophone, the alkaline battery, the motion-picture camera and the carbon transmitter, which facilitated the use of Bell's telephone.

One story goes that, when interviewed about the huge number of failures that he'd encountered while trying to invent the storage battery – apparently about 50 000 before achieving any results – Thomas Edison replied, 'Results? Why, I have gotten a lot of results. I know fifty thousand things that won't work!'

The medical superman: Christopher Reeve (1952–2004), actor

After breaking his neck while horse riding in 1995, Christopher Reeve was told that he would die a quadriplegic (*The New Yorker*, 2003). Not one to give up, he was determined to walk again and began to fund research into the use of special equipment that could help paralysed animals regain their mobility by putting their limbs through the motions of movement. Many people were sceptical, but in 2003 Reeve was given an award for 'heroic advocacy of medical research in general and victims of a disability in particular'. In his acceptance speech, Reeve remarked that the award had offered him 'encouragement to be even more annoying and difficult in the future!'

The musician: Wolfgang Amadeus Mozart (1756–1791)

From the age of three, Mozart began to play the keyboard. He started lessons at four and composed his own pieces from six. His early works were frequently arrangements of works by other composers, and his first original concerto to be regarded as a masterpiece was not written until he was 21. While this may sound extraordinarily young, by that time he had been composing concertos for ten years and he had put in an absolutely vast amount of practice.

Malcolm Gladwell (2008), author of *Outliers: The Story of Success*, quotes neurologist Daniel Levitin, who suggests that 'ten thousand hours of practice is required to achieve the level of mastery associated with being a world-class expert – in anything'. Gladwell goes on to say: 'Even

Mozart – the greatest musical prodigy of all time – couldn't hit his stride until he had his ten thousand hours in. Practice isn't the thing you do once you're good. It's the thing you do that makes you good.'

The X-Factor: Simon Cowell (b. 1959)

Cowell left school/technical college at 17 with just three O levels and – knowing he wanted to be in the music business – was prepared to start at the very bottom with a job in the mail room of EMI Music Publishing. After working his way up to the department that places songs with major artists, he left to form his own company, E&S Music. A difficult and unsuccessful year later, making the decision to cut his losses and move on, he left E&S and joined with a new partner to launch their own record label – Fanfare Records. From there, he moved on to BMB, signing new artists and astonishing the industry with his persistence in pursuing his instincts, even when they seemed to conflict with popular opinion. In the last few years, he has been involved in numerous shows such as *Pop Idol*, *The X-Factor* and *Britain's Got Talent*, and continues to work on new projects now, even though highly successful (Cowell: 2003).

The politician: Abraham Lincoln (1809–1865)

- Failed in business (age 22)
- Ran for Legislature – defeated (age 23)

- Again failed in business (age 24)
- Elected to Legislature (age 25)
- Sweetheart died (age 26)
- Had a nervous breakdown (age 27)
- Lost bid to become House Speaker (age 29)
- Defeated for Elector (age 31)
- Defeated for Congress (age 34)
- Elected to Congress (age 37)
- Lost re-election bid (age 39)
- Son died (age 41)
- Ran for Senate and lost (age 46)
- Defeated for Vice President (age 47)
- Ran for Senate again – and lost (age 49)
- Elected President of the United States (age 51)

The author: J. K. Rowling (b. 1965)

When J.K. Rowling wrote the first Harry Potter book in 1995, it was rejected by 12 different publishers (Zeleznock, 2008). Apparently, even Bloomsbury, the small publishing house that finally purchased Rowling's manuscript, told the author to 'get a day job'. Rowling is currently the second-richest female entertainer in the world (Oprah Winfrey nabbing the top spot), but life was very difficult for her at the beginning. Despite a divorce, the death of her mother and the fact that she was living with her daughter in a tiny flat on government subsidies, she didn't give up, instead devoting most of her spare time to writing.

The entrepreneur: Harland Sanders (1890–1980)

(This story can be found at **www.anecdotage.com/index.php? aid=8379**)

At the age of 63, Harland Sanders was offered nearly $200 000 for the restaurant–motel–service station business he'd built up over the years. Not feeling ready to retire yet, he turned down the offer – only to find that in two years' time the government had built a new motorway that bypassed his business. Within a year he lost everything.

Now flat broke and living on government benefits, he decided to try to persuade someone to fund him in his plan to open a restaurant that specialised in cooked chicken. He took his battered old car, a pressure cooker and his special recipe to restaurant after restaurant, suffering 300 rejections before he found someone who believed in him.

A few years later, he opened the first of what would become thousands of successful restaurants located around the world. Known by his nickname, 'Colonel Sanders', he is the legend behind Kentucky Fried Chicken.

The film director: Walt Disney (1901–1966)

Fired from the newspaper where he worked because his boss thought he lacked creativity, Walt Disney formed his own animation company called Laugh-O-Gram Films in 1921 (Zeleznock, 2008). He worked hard to raise money to support the business, but unfortunately when his New York distributer went out of business he was forced to close his own company. At that point, the story goes that he was so poor he even resorted to eating dog food.

Spending his last dollars on a train ticket to Hollywood, Disney began to create cartoon characters and films. It was a struggle, though. He was told that Mickey Mouse would fail because the mouse would 'terrify women', *The Three Little Pigs* was rejected because it needed more characters, and *Pinocchio* was shut down during production and Disney had to rewrite the entire storyline.

When Disney tried to make the book *Mary Poppins* into a film in 1944, its author refused to sell him the rights. It took more than 15 years of persuasion and visits to the author's home in England before she finally gave him permission to bring *Mary Poppins* to the big screen. The result is a timeless classic.

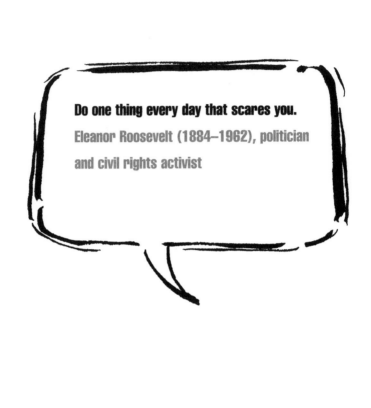

Do one thing every day that scares you.

Eleanor Roosevelt (1884–1962), politician and civil rights activist

9 HOW TO TAKE THE RIGHT SORT OF RISK

The good news is that we're not talking about risking life and limb in the pursuit of dangerous sports – or even staying up late to watch a TV programme and hoping the teacher won't notice that the homework's not been done properly. What is at issue here is developing the willingness to move outside one's comfort zone and to try something new, even when success isn't guaranteed. It's also about going out on a limb and putting forward the wacky idea or the controversial opinion regardless of the possibility that you'll be laughed out of the room.

These days we tend to wrap our kids up in cotton wool, to try to protect them from every possible danger – with the result that they don't learn that sometimes it's right to take a *considered* risk, to weigh things up, envisage the best and worst possible outcomes, recognise that we might end up getting it wrong/looking stupid/feeling scared – and then to *go for it anyway*.

Recently I was leading a session on risk with a large group of 12-year-olds. Towards the end, they each had to note down one risk that they'd like to take – one thing that perhaps they were a bit scared of doing but that they had a hunch might have a really positive impact on them. They wrote down the best thing that could happen if they took that risk, the worst thing that could happen and then what might happen if they *didn't* take the risk. The response was amazing – and revealing. So many of their dreams were perfectly achievable. Apart from the occasional visionary who wanted to climb Mount Everest during the Easter holiday or run for London Mayor at the next election, the risks they described were almost worryingly tame. It reminded me of a statistic that came out recently – that one in four children between the ages of eight and ten has never played outside unsupervised (Frean, 2008). We need to find ways of increasing the level of risk in our children's lives – obviously gently and within reasonable limits – so that they learn to recognise the feelings and thought processes that are involved.

When pushed to the very edge of what you can do, you learn much more and much more quickly. What's more, you learn that failure or other people's negative reactions are not the end of the world – which is an important thing for children to realise. Some children are absolutely crippled with a fear of failing. At school, they select less challenging tasks and options to ensure that they maintain the grades and praise they have come to need; at home, they avoid new experiences that they might have come to love or that would have developed their character in ways they will never discover.

Developing a healthy attitude towards risk and the resilience to bounce back when the result is not what you hoped is a vital part of growing up and of achieving one's intellectual, physical and emotional potential. It's something that separates the truly successful from those who never dare to take a chance.

As Simon Woodroffe, founder of YO! Sushi and a judge on the BBC show *Dragons' Den*, said, '*We need to encourage children to push themselves, to go beyond their limits, in order to build a nation of bold and confident people … Helping children to experience risks in a managed way is not only key to their general development but also to bringing on the next generation of entrepreneurs, to the benefit of the economy and society as a whole*' (Bennett, 2008).

Quick tips

✓ **Encourage thoughtful risk-taking.** Guide your child towards new challenges and steer them away from the 'play it safe' route whenever it's appropriate. I'm not suggesting anything wildly dangerous – simply that we need to look out for potentially interesting activities and valuable experiences that are just that bit beyond what our children normally and comfortably do.

✓ **Support your children through these experiences.** Encourage them, be with them, believe in them massively and let this show, but stand back at the end and they'll feel fantastic when they succeed in overcoming their fears. And when they don't, help them learn that it's not the end of the world. The very nature of risk means that the outcome will be unexpected – sometimes better, sometimes worse than hoped. What matters is that they had a go and they're the stronger for it.

✓ Help your children work out for themselves whether a risk is too great. Show empathy for their situation, for example by saying 'I can see that sounds fun ... What are the good points?. What are the bad points?' Teach them to consider how it supports or conflicts with their values - things like honesty, kindness and responsibility. Above all, make sure you do this for situations where taking the risk is the right outcome as well as for cases where the cons outweigh the pros - otherwise the exercise will become linked with saying no. If your child wants to take what you think is an unwise risk, stop to check your own reasoning before leaping in with a blanket 'No!' Are you automatically right - or might you be overprotecting him or her?

✓ **Praise your child for taking a chance, for being brave and for showing initiative.** Do this particularly when the outcome is apparently unsuccessful. Point out how much more admirable it is to take a responsible risk than to be the type who waits timidly for others to have the adventures.

✓ **Explain to your child how important it is that they seek advice if ever they are not sure what to do about a risk they are considering.** Help them to be very clear about

who they can approach – and
suggest alternatives if a
situation arises where they'd
rather not talk to you about
something.

✓ **Most importantly, take risks
yourself.** As adults, we forget
how nerve-wracking it is to try
new things and we move
through most days firmly in
our comfort zone. And when
we don't – when we have to
put ourselves on the line and
run the risk of getting things
wrong and looking stupid – it's
rarely our children we tell
about it. Your child needs to
see you trying out new things,
overcoming your fear and not

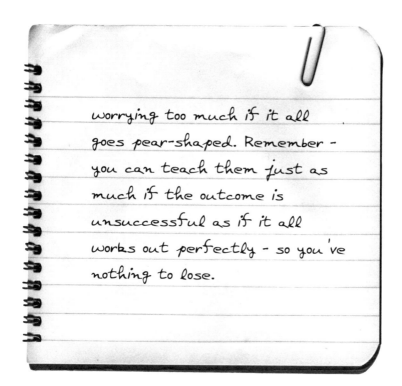

worrying too much if it all
goes pear-shaped. Remember -
you can teach them just as
much if the outcome is
unsuccessful as if it all
works out perfectly - so you've
nothing to lose.

Activities and games

You could try ...

THE RISK INVESTIGATOR

Encourage your child to see whether they can find any examples of characters in books or films who have taken a risk, then weigh up whether they thought these risks were 'worth it' or not.

Extend this to look out for stories of people in real life – at school, in the family, in the news – who have taken risks. It's really interesting to link this with an investigation into your family tree, as this personal link brings the concept of risk-taking closer to home.

RISKOMETER

This idea was devised by Professor Guy Claxton, a leading educationalist who has developed a school programme called 'Building Learning Power' that aims to tackle the sort of issues described in this book. He suggests creating a 'riskometer' – which could be displayed somewhere in the house and which could record the risks your child has taken. It might look something like a height chart – with a scale that you and your child could decide on together (for

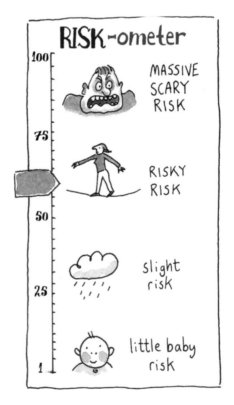

example, from 'little baby risk' to 'massive scary risk').

Whenever a risk arises that your child feels (and you agree) is right to take, get them to decide beforehand where on the scale it should go. When they take the step and 'go for it', they could write it on a piece of paper or draw a picture to illustrate it – then stick it on the scale as a reminder of their bravery. Both risks that pay off and those that don't should be celebrated.

KEEP A RISK RECORD

Another option is to encourage your child to keep a risk record. This could take the form of a diary, with a page devoted to each special risk that your child would like to take – whether it's auditioning for a play, trying out for a team, inviting a new friend over, volunteering to be involved in a new venture, overcoming a fear or expressing an opinion on something about which they feel strongly. They could note what they'd ideally like to do, list what the best and the worst outcomes might be, and maybe even illustrate it with a picture. If they decide the risk is worth taking, then a time limit could be set and a record kept afterwards of what happened.

Imagine how great this would be! You'd be bringing your child up with such a healthy attitude towards life – developing the habit of carefully thinking things through, and the courage to take the plunge when the risk seems right. Of course, what would make this even more powerful would be if you were willing to keep a risk record yourself as well!

PERSONAL MOTTOS

As with persistence, this is an area where there are all sorts of fantastically inspiring quotes. Turn them into posters and pick one to be your own personal motto. You never know, your kids may follow suit ...

Here are three to get you started:

> 'It is not because things are difficult that we do not dare, it is because we do not dare that they are difficult' – *Seneca (c.4 BC – AD 65), Roman Stoic philosopher*.

> 'Life shrinks or expands in proportion to one's courage' – *Anais Nin (1903–1977), author*.

> 'You miss 100 per cent of the shots you never take' – *Wayne Gretzky (b. 1961), coach of the Phoenix Coyotes and retired Canadian professional ice-hockey player*.

TAKING RISKS WITH FRIENDS

Encourage your child to invite new friends over every now and then – not just the people they know well and usually play with. It may not always be wildly successful, but it's a really good way of helping them learn to take a risk with social situations. And it may result in some unexpected friendships. Chat together afterwards about how they feel it went. Was the risk worth it?

TAKING RISKS WITH FOOD

Food offers a really good chance to help your child learn about taking risks within a very safe context. Lots of people will tell you that cooking with your children is a worthwhile activity, but the emphasis on slavishly following a set recipe means that a wonderful creative opportunity is being lost. Children spend so much time already following instructions: although this is certainly a skill they need to know, why not change your approach every now and then?

Start by telling them that one of the greatest chefs of all time is Heston Blumenthal, proprietor of The Fat Duck, voted in 2005 as 'the best restaurant in the world' by the '50 Best' Academy of over 600 international food critics, journalists and chefs. Sometimes described as a 'culinary alchemist', Blumenthal is the ultimate risk-taker when it comes to food. Breaking through traditional conventions, he experiments – very precisely and scientifically – to seek highly innovative new taste combinations that others wouldn't even dream of trying. The result: cauliflower risotto with chocolate jelly, scrambled egg and bacon ice cream, salmon poached in liquorice gel, mango and Douglas fir puree and, possibly his most famous dish, snail porridge!

Encourage your child to be a culinary risk-taker next time you're cooking together. This could either be by following a recipe but then adapting it slightly – varying the quantities or substituting a different ingredient to see what happens – or, if you're feeling really brave, by allowing them to create their own entirely new 'Blumenthal' dish. There are only two rules:

- They have to record their recipe – ingredients and instructions – as they go along (just in case they create something truly magnificent, you can tell them).

■—■ They – and you – must not only try the final product but also critically assess it.

This means both of you acting as food critics and talking about what's good and bad about the taste that has been created – which could, of course, be a lot of fun.

If your child turns out to have a real flair for this, why not get them to put together their own cookery book? Now that could be an interesting Christmas present for the grandparents ...

And another thought!

 You may want to keep the scale small to minimise wastage. While this activity may seem extravagant, viewing the ingredients as craft activities can help!

One potentially useful spin-off might be that this sort of activity, if done from an early age, could help to minimise the sort of fussiness about food that some children (and subsequently, their parents) suffer from.

INITIATIVE ROLE MODEL: STEVEN SPIELBERG (B. 1946)

You can use this story about Steven Spielberg, the American film director, to demonstrate the benefits of a fearless nature and a bit of initiative. The story comes from a *Time* magazine article on **www.anecdotage.com/index.php?aid=14372**.

At the age of 17, Steven Spielberg took the studio tour of Universal Pictures. During a break, he crept away from the group and wandered off on his own. He got chatting to a man, who turned out to be the head of the editorial department and who agreed to look at some of the short films Spielberg had been making. The next day, when Spielberg showed the man some of his films, the man was very impressed but said he didn't have the authority to issue him with any more passes to visit the studios.

Spielberg recognised this was his opportunity and took an enormous risk: without a pass, he turned up the following day, wearing a smart suit and carrying a briefcase (containing, apparently, nothing but a sandwich and some chocolate bars). He waved at the guard, who let him through. He did this each day that summer, spending time with directors, editors and writers. He found an office that wasn't being used and moved in, adding his name to the list of occupants: Steven Spielberg, Room 23C.

He went on to direct films such as *Jaws* (1975), the *Indiana Jones* films (1981, 1984, 1989), *ET the Extra-Terrestrial* (1982) and *Lost World: Jurassic Park II* (1997).

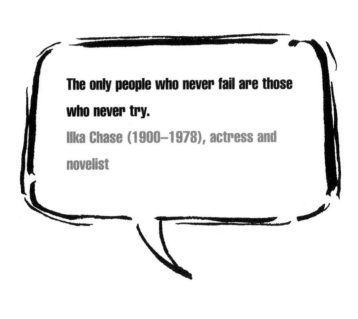

The only people who never fail are those who never try.
Ilka Chase (1900–1978), actress and novelist

10 HOW TO LEARN FROM FAILURE AS WELL AS SUCCESS

Life is about experimenting – and the most interesting and worthwhile experiments will more often go wrong than right! We need to teach our children that, although success is of course good news, failure is absolutely natural too – especially for the adventurous, the daring, and the ones who are willing to learn, to take a chance and to put themselves out there. Far better to be someone like that than someone boring who never dares to try at all.

You may have a difficult job on your hands here, though, as what you're saying will probably seem to your child to contradict their experience. Generally, at school, getting something wrong is seen as the *opposite of* getting it right (you get a cross and a lower mark) rather than as a vital step in the right direction. Even when teachers do their best to use a mistake to help their pupils learn, it's hard for children to avoid the impression that it's the one who gets things right all the time who gets the most praise and admiration.

I like to think of real achievement as a set of stairs: the rise is the period of failure, the tread is the plateau of success. If our lives were constant success, then we wouldn't climb. We wouldn't get anywhere worth going. The most interesting people are the ones who've failed most often, because they are the ones who have been brave enough to keep on finding new experiences to try, and new challenges that will really stretch them. People who coast along seemingly succeeding all the time are almost certainly not achieving as highly as they could, because they're never putting their neck on the line.

Ideally we want our children to recognise that, at some point or other, we all get things wrong and that it doesn't necessarily reflect a particular weakness. Sometimes it's just life's unpredictability. And where it *is* our fault – where we did have a part to play – then the best thing to do is to learn from it. Analyse it, reflect on it. What went wrong? Why hadn't I anticipated that? How could I change my approach next time? As Mary Kay Ash, founder of the hugely successful Mary Kay Cosmetics, said, *'For every failure, there's an alternative course of action. You just have to find it. When you come to a roadblock, take a detour.'*

It's this process that really sets the high achiever apart from the rest. It's often called being 'resilient'. When things go pear-shaped, will we stay down or will we pick ourselves back up? Will we hide away, feeling hurt, or will we try to come up with a better idea or a more ingenious solution? Will we learn from our mistakes, or will we keep making the same ones over and over again?

'A man's errors are his portals of discovery,' James Joyce said. And, more recently, Sir Ken Robinson, a leading expert in creativity, observed: *'If you're not prepared to be wrong, you'll never come up with anything original.'*

As children get older, some become absolutely paralysed by a fear of failure and, as such, steer clear of new challenges that might show them up. What a terrible condition we've inflicted on them! As parents and teachers, we really need to do something about this if today's young people are going to have a chance to achieve all they can achieve in life.

Quick tips

✓ Introduce, as early as
possible, the idea that it's
better to fail at something
difficult than succeed at
something easy - because what
does the latter teach you?
One takes you a step forward;
the other simply reinforces
the position you're in.

✓ When you're chatting with
your child after school,
instead of just asking about
what went well, ask them
every now and then what they
failed at. This way, failure
can be seen as a matter-of-
fact part of life - something
we all go through. Help your
child open up by telling them

about your own examples –
what did you get wrong?
Where did you fail to achieve
what you wanted to? And
what are you going to do about
it? Is it a situation where you
simply need to try again? Or
one where you're going to have
to change tack and try a new
approach? What do you know
now that you didn't know
before? This is really
important, as otherwise your
child is likely to continue to
believe that failing is just for
children, for the inexperienced
and for the unsuccessful.

✓ **Let your child fail.** Our
instinct so often is to stop our

children making mistakes - to catch them before they fall, to step in before it all goes wrong. And, of course, often that may well be the best approach. But not always. Because otherwise it makes mistakes all the more terrifying in prospect and all the more dreadful when they finally happen (as they will). The only way your children will learn a positive attitude towards mistakes is by making a good number of them.

✓ **When failure happens, judge how to respond.** Sometimes a simple 'Oh well, never mind' or 'These things happen' will do -

deliberately light-hearted to show that it's not the end of the world. At other times - especially if it was something that really mattered to them - once the sympathy stage is over, help your child to think back over the steps they took that led to that failure. What could they do differently next time? Rather like a detective, find out what secret clue they now know that means they're a step closer to succeeding next time.

✓ Teach your children how to accept constructive criticism. Help them realise that it's natural for this to 'hurt' and give them some practical strategies for dealing with it: staying calm, taking two or three slow deep breaths, listening carefully and looking out for what they can learn from it. Tell them, if you can, about situations when you've had to deal with this yourself.

✓ Help your child find a method that works for them when dealing with disappointment. For some kids it may be to talk it through, but others might need a practical outlet, such as sport, climbing or walking the dog.

Activities and games

You could try ...

GOOD SIDE, BAD SIDE

When something goes wrong, make it a routine that you always do a 'good side, bad side' analysis, by asking:

- What was the bad side of this going wrong? You could use this as a chance to be sympathetic and to help your child recognise the different factors that contributed to the failure – their own lack of planning, foresight or tact, the role of other people, bad luck, etc.

- What might be the good side? Encourage your child to think creatively: is there *anything* good that could come out of this? Could it help them come up with better ideas or plans for next time? Might there be some unexpected bonus, for example a new friendship or the chance to do something special to put the situation right?

Reaffirm your belief in your child, with clear reasons. For example, you might say: 'You're a creative person, I know you'll come up with an idea for how to put this right' or 'You rarely give up on things – if you decide to stick with this, I bet things will improve ...'

COMPUTER GAMES

Computer games are a perfect model for the very best attitude to both success and failure. Children seem naturally to expect that they won't get past each new level without real persistence, and getting blasted to death or thrown back to the start just doesn't seem to bother them. Sure, it's a bit frustrating, but they know they're getting better each time.

When you next spot your child gritting their teeth with determination over the latest game, praise them for demonstrating such a great attitude. Point out that it's exactly this that makes certain people successful in life – and show that you're impressed that they're already well on the way. When the moment is right (*not* while they're immersed in the game!), see if you can begin a conversation where you try to think of other situations in life when their sort of computer-game resilience would be useful.

SPORT

Sport offers a great chance to develop positive attitudes. Although success feels fantastic, it's only worth celebrating if the other team or individual really puts up a fight. If there's no challenge, there's no point. If your child wins at something, don't just say 'Well done'; ask them how good the other team was. If they had particular strengths, how did your child's side overcome them?

GAMES EVENINGS

Consider having a weekly games evening, where you and your children spend time playing traditional board games, card games or even occasionally computer games. There are lots of games on the market that are great for developing character traits such as persistence, risk-taking and resilience, as well as providing opportunities to practise decision-making and problem-solving skills. To get the most out of these evenings, try (subtly, if possible) to draw attention to this. The fact that you're getting involved yourself gives you the perfect opportunity to drop in comments such as:

- Well done! You took a risk – so it didn't pay off that time, but sometimes it's the right thing to do.
- I'm so impressed at how you're not giving up! That shows real strength.
- Oh, I can't believe I've been sent back to the beginning! I really feel like giving up now. I'm not going to let this beat me though – OK, start again.

You may think of other ways to reinforce the character traits we've been looking at. For instance, to help build a positive attitude towards failure, when playing board games you could have two winning titles – one for the person who won the game and one for the person who can think of the best new tip for someone playing it next time.

Children love playing games, and my experience is that this is something that's really slipped out of family life. And yet an hour playing games like this with your child is surely better than racing off to yet another after-school activity – and it certainly beats television.

And another thought!

 Just to get you started, here are a few of the games I've found that work really well for this sort of event:

- *Rush Hour* or *Safari Rush Hour*, *Hoppers* or *Heroes Hoppers* – by Ravensburger

- *Gridworks* – by ThinkFun
- *Pagoda Challenge* – by Square Root Games
- *SET* – by SET enterprises
- *Blokus* – by Green Board Games
- *Tantrix* – by Family Games/Tantrix

And, of course, the old favourites such as *Cluedo* (now repackaged under the name of *Clue*, by Parker Brothers) and *Monopoly* (Hasbro) are wonderful if you have the time.

JUMBLED QUOTES

As with the earlier chapters on persistence and risk-taking, there are some really inspiring quotes out there that can help to convey a positive approach to success and failure. Again, you could simply ask your child to pick one or two and help you make them into posters – or, if you're looking for a different angle, you could say you've found a puzzle on the Internet (it's only a small fib) and it's really bugging you. You've been given a famous quote but it's chopped up into two-word (and occasional three-word) pieces and you need their help to work it out.

Write or photocopy the examples opposite on to separate pieces of paper and get your child to reassemble them for you and then stick them on to a bigger piece of paper to create a poster for you. Answers overleaf!

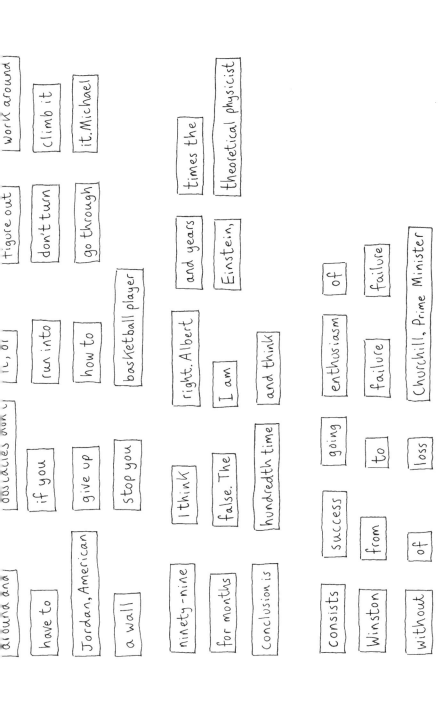

Here are the answers to three 'jumbled quotes' on the previous page:

> 'Obstacles don't have to stop you. If you run into a wall, don't turn around and give up. Figure out how to climb it, go through it, or work around it' – *Michael Jordan, American basketball player*.

> 'I think and think for months and years. Ninety-nine times the conclusion is false. The hundredth time I am right' – *Albert Einstein, theoretical physicist*.

> 'Success consists of going from failure to failure without loss of enthusiasm' – *Winston Churchill, prime minister*.

THREE TOP TIPS FOR TESTS AND EXAMS

1   Shift the focus away from 'exams as a means of judging you' towards 'exams as a way of helping you to learn'. Bring up your child to know that the purpose of exams is to give them the opportunity to 'show off' what they've learnt, while also identifying areas where they need more help.

2   When the tests are over and the grades are in, whether your child has achieved a successful result or has not done as well as hoped, it's worth helping them to consider *why* this happened. If they did well, what was their secret? What clever steps did they take? If the result was lower than expected, was it something that was out of their hands, such as feeling ill that day or getting questions they hadn't covered? Or, when they look back, was there something wrong with the approach they took? One idea is to get them to draw

up an action plan for next time or a 'secrets to success' guide for a younger brother or sister. It doesn't need to be too serious. It could have a title such as 'How not to fail at science', with speech bubbles and cartoon illustrations if your child enjoys drawing.

3   If you want to praise or reward your child, do so for their effort, their attitude and their own personal progress, rather than fixing on concrete results. It has been shown that students with 'learning goals' rather than 'performance goals' do much better in the longer run. When they get something wrong, their world does not collapse – instead, they have a reason to find out why they failed in that area and what they could do to improve next time.

Believe nothing, no matter where you read it, or who said it, no matter if I have said it, unless it agrees with your own reason and your own common sense.

Buddha (*c.*563–483 BC)

11 HOW TO SORT SENSE FROM NONSENSE

Ideas, proposals, arguments, recommendations, opinions . . . we are constantly bombarded by them in newspapers, on the television and Internet, in shops and advertisements, even from our own friends and family. A valuable indication of a free and vibrant society on the one hand, but a little overwhelming sometimes on the other.

No wonder we worry about our children. Kids today face real pressure from all sorts of sources and even those who look street-wise rarely have had the chance to develop real skills to help them work out what and who to believe. One of the most important qualities we can teach our children is how not to be gullible, how to deal critically with what they hear and read. This doesn't mean being negative. What it involves is learning to weigh up different points of view, to check the quality of the reasoning and evidence that is being offered and to reach an opinion that's supported by clear thinking – otherwise known as sorting sense from nonsense, as this chapter's title suggests.

Back in the eighteenth century, Edmund Burke (1729–1797), a political theorist and philosopher, said that *'To read without reflecting is like eating without digesting'.* Sound advice – but things have moved on. Our children need to surf the Internet, navigate chatrooms, screen emails, see through adverts, weigh up the blogs and scour the small print. It's a huge feast and they'll get more than indigestion if they don't learn how to think for themselves.

The first few activities suggested below are useful to introduce younger children to some of the underlying concepts needed to form a truly logical approach: recognising the difference between definite, probable and possible conclusions and between fact and opinion, for instance. This leads on to specific tools and techniques that will help equip children when deciding for themselves what to believe.

It would take a whole book to tackle this area properly. This chapter merely provides a start.

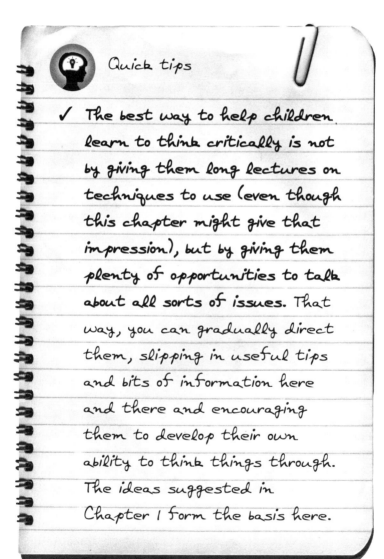

Quick tips

✓ The best way to help children learn to think critically is not by giving them long lectures on techniques to use (even though this chapter might give that impression), but by giving them plenty of opportunities to talk about all sorts of issues. That way, you can gradually direct them, slipping in useful tips and bits of information here and there and encouraging them to develop their own ability to think things through. The ideas suggested in Chapter 1 form the basis here.

✓ Go online for some great sites
for parents offering detailed
advice and guidance about
Internet safety.
Recommended sites include
www.bbc.co.uk/chatguide/ and
www.wisekids.org.uk/
parents.htm.

✓ When, as parents, we model a
sceptical outlook, it doesn't
have to take all the fun out
of everything. Instead of
telling your child what you
believe and don't believe, leave
some room for intelligent
uncertainty. Suggest that
you're not quite sure what
you think about a particular
topic and invite your child to

come up with a few possible views themselves. Learning and skill-forming are most likely to take place where there is room to think and grow.

✓ Sorting sense from nonsense ultimately hinges on being able to think of and assess alternative explanations. This is a habit that can be practised in all sorts of situations. Whether you're listening to the radio, reading a bedtime story or out walking and you spot something unusual, you'll find there are often occasions where you and your child can have fun

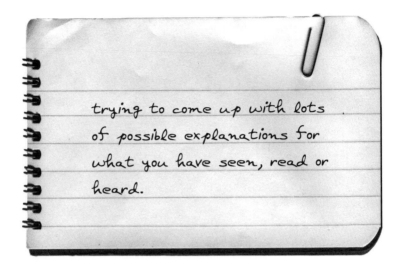

trying to come up with lots of possible explanations for what you have seen, read or heard.

Activities and games

You could try ...

THE UNCERTAINTY SPECTRUM

Young children find it quite difficult to distinguish things that are definite from those that are merely probable. Similarly, the difference between impossible and unlikely is also a baffler. It's useful, therefore, to bring these words into discussions about everyday situations. Begin with an object of some type – it may be a building you're walking past or the food that you're eating. Can you take it in turns to come up with five things that are definitely true about it? How about five things that are completely impossible?

As your child grows familiar with these concepts, introduce words to convey the spectrum in between: 'unlikely', 'possible', 'probable' and so on. For example, it's fun to invite your child to come up with ten things that are unlikely to happen tomorrow. Draw a line across a piece of paper and label one end 'impossible' and the other 'definite'. As your child suggests each event, get them to think about where on the line it would fall. Some funny discussions follow (as well as a seriously good introduction to probability), as your child ends up trying to work out whether aliens invading the planet is more or less likely than their teacher coming to school on an elephant.

And another thought!

If you're up for it, it's great fun to make this really practical by hanging up a washing line and writing each suggestion on to a piece of paper. These can then be clipped on to the line and moved around as each new argument is put forwad. Or use sticky notes and stick them along the edge of a table or window.

GUESS WHAT?

People often try to convince us to believe a particular conclusion, which they present as being either (a) definitely true, or (b) the only possible option, or (c) both (a) and (b). This is something children need to learn to watch out for – especially given that such conclusions are, in reality, very rare.

Catch your child's interest with a surprising fact, such as 'Guess what? Koalas sleep for 22 hours a day.' (A list of such facts can easily be generated through a quick search on the Internet.) Then draw your child into a reflective discussion, by saying something like 'Isn't that amazing? I wonder what it means ... I suppose it might be true, therefore, that koalas are the laziest animals in the world' or 'Perhaps it might be true that for the other two hours a day they race around so fast that it wears them out'!

Take it in turns to draw further possible conclusions, using the starter phrase 'It might be true that ...'. Which are the most likely theories? Which are the least likely? As with the activity above, you might like to try to place these hypotheses on a spectrum, from least to most plausible.

Then try some definite conclusions, using the starter phrase 'It *must* be true that ...' This is much harder – it stumps a lot of adults when I try it on them. Treat all attempts positively, gently questioning your child to see whether they are sure that what they said is *definitely* true.

Point out how hard it is to draw a definite conclusion and mention that it's a good idea to double-check when someone says something is definitely true. This might lead – when the time is right – to a discussion about your child's experiences at school. Do their friends ever try to persuade them that they *have to* do something or that something is *definitely* true? How could they respond to this? Might there be other possible actions that could be taken or beliefs that could be held?

OPEN EYES, OPEN MIND

This is a really good way of developing better observation and deduction skills – and you can be pretty much anywhere to use it. It works well as an activity for two or more people, with players taking it in turns to give three answers – one for each question below. By answering the string of three questions all in one turn, it encourages the players to follow through a particular observation and line of thought.

- Give me one thing that's definitely true about ... [that painting/those people/this street].
- Now give me one thing that might be true about ... How do you know this?
- Can you think of something you wish you knew about ... ?

CRAZY CONCLUSIONS

This requires an adult or older sibling to come up with a statement that contains an implausible conclusion. For example:

- It rained today; therefore there will be a flood.
- Tigers are dangerous; therefore we should get rid of all the tigers in the world.

Alice is going to buy all her friends a present each; therefore she must have won the lottery.

It's great fun to present the statement with a mock serious face, as if you really believe it. Ask your child whether they agree. If they don't, pretend to look horrified – they think you're wrong? Encourage them to explain what is wrong with your reasoning. Then play a game where you both come up with as many plausible conclusions as possible.

SU DOKUS

Su doku puzzles are a great way of reinforcing the difference between what is definitely true and what is possibly true. It's vital to teach your child that the puzzle will fail if they rely on guessing – even if they are making what seems to be a good guess. The only way to win is by drawing logical deductions – by working out what *must* be true.

FACT *V.* OPINION

It's worth spending some time helping your child to recognise the difference between things that are factually true and statements that merely reflect a person's opinion. This can be linked to the observation skills game 'Five things you spot about …' on p. 42. Once a subject has been selected by one player – such as the car in front of you if you're stuck in a traffic jam – the other person must describe five things they wouldn't immediately have noticed about that object.

For this version, you could add the rule that these five

observations must be factually accurate – they must be things that you both can see and verify. This could then be followed with three opinions about the object, using the starter phrase 'In my opinion ...' each time.

This game is more challenging than it sounds and can be played at different levels with children of different ages.

WHAT DO YOU BELIEVE BUT CANNOT PROVE?

This game is a healthy counter-balance to all this logic! It's worth pointing out to your child that many of us hold beliefs that cannot be supported by watertight evidence or backed up with flawless logic. And yet we still hold them – and this isn't necessarily a bad thing. In many ways, it's what makes us human. I've had some wonderful discussions with older students, prompted by the question 'What do you believe but cannot prove?' Try it with your children – it's fascinating!

THINKING CRITICALLY ABOUT THE NEWS

As children get older, introduce them to the need to think critically about what they hear and read. Point out that, unfortunately, not everything we hear comes to us in a form that is completely true and accurate. However, the good side of this is that it makes understanding the world more like a game. Some people are simply gullible and believe everything they're told. However, your child might like to learn some of the tricks that adults use so they can 'catch them out' and decide for themselves what to believe. (You get the idea of the sort of language to use!)

Chapter 5 introduced some strategies you might like to try to encourage your child to get excited about what's going on in the world. It's a good idea to watch out for articles and letters that deal with topics in which you know your child is interested.

Let's say that you or your child has found a really interesting article (which should be short and snappy until they're a fair bit older, otherwise you'll put them off). Here are three 'magic questions' you could teach them to ask:

- What is the main point that the reporter is making? What does he or she really want me to believe?
- What reasons have they given for this?
- How good are these reasons? Are they persuasive or can I spot any problems with them? [See below for a brief look at statistics, credibility issues and favourite fallacies.]

In doing this, you are encouraging your child to see themselves as a 'critical thinker' – someone with the intelligence to decide for themselves whether they agree or disagree with the opinion or evidence that's being presented.

___

WHO CAN YOU TRUST?

Assessing whether to believe a particular source requires some awareness of its credibility. Children will not acquire this knowledge without some guidance – so it's worth teaching them the following six criteria to apply (and the associated RAVENS mnemonic):

Reputation – does the person/organisation/newspaper/ website have a good reputation?

Ability to see/hear – was the evidence collected by someone who was in a good position to see/hear what happened?

Vested interest – might the source have something to gain by presenting a particular point of view?

Expertise – is the evidence being offered by someone who knows what they're talking about?

Neutrality – is there a chance that the information might be biased without the person realising it?

Selectivity – does the information represent the whole story?

The aim is that this eventually becomes a familiar part of your child's thinking when reading a newspaper or viewing a website.

SHOCK STATISTICS

Newspapers sometimes contain surprising statistics that offer a good starting point for interesting discussions. For instance, did you know that ...

'The average Briton now spends a quarter of his or her waking hours on the phone, using email or sending text messages' – *Daily Mail.*

'The average person watched nearly 4 hours of television a day in 2008 or 26 hours and 18 minutes per week' – *The Daily Telegraph.*

'UK householders throw away one third of all the food they buy' – *The Independent.*

When you come up against a statistic that you think your child might find intriguing, the secret is to present it in such a way that your child feels you are genuinely surprised and amazed by your finding. Introduce it with something like: 'Wow! You'll never guess what I've just discovered. Would you believe that ...?'

Then, in the course of the discussion that you hope will follow, you could ask your child:

- Whether he or she is also surprised by the statistic. If so, why?
- Whether he or she thinks any action should be taken as a result of it. What would they do if they were in charge of the organisation/country/world?
- To have a go – with you – at drawing some definite or possible conclusions from this evidence. You could take it in turns to try to complete either of the sentences: 'Therefore it *must* be true that ...' or 'Therefore it *might* be true that ...'
- Whether they trust the statistic. How do they think the information was collected? Might there be any reasons not to take it at surface value? For instance, can we be sure that enough data were gathered to make them representative? Linked to this, if it is a poll of some type, were the people asked sufficiently varied to reflect a general consensus? You could have fun with your child coming up with examples of clearly biased statistics – for instance, '98 per cent of readers of *Paranormal Post* believe in ghosts'.
- To imagine (or even draw) a cartoon that would illustrate the statistic.

Several 'fallacies' – errors in reasoning – are described below. However, one that is particularly relevant when dealing with statistics goes by the fancy title of 'ad populem' or 'the bandwagon fallacy'. Basically, this covers those instances when someone uses the fact that a proposition has lots of support as a reason for accepting it. It's the classic, 'Lots of people believe in horoscopes so they must be true' sort of argument. Unfortunately – unless supported by clear reasons and relevant experience – lots of people can be very wrong.

CATCH THEM OUT!

Here are a few more favourite fallacies that often creep into people's reasoning. Although the examples below are illustrated with less than serious comments, they represent genuine and quite deceptive 'tricks' that adults often use (either intentionally or accidentally) when arguing. Listen to virtually any radio interview and you're bound to find one of them. It works well to present these to your child as ways in which they can look smart and catch adults out.

It's not fair! (tu quoque)

What does it entail? Arguing that just because someone else gets away with it, so should you.

Playground example: 'But Sarah's mum lets her go out on her own late at night so why can't I?'

Grown-ups' example: 'Everyone bends the truth on their online dating profile, so it's OK for me to say I'm in administration rather than my company is.'

How to fight back: 'Does that make it right? Are the situations really just the same?'

Be rude! (ad hominem)

What does it entail? Attacking the person rather than getting to grips with what they are actually saying.

Playground example: 'Don't listen to him, he smells!'

Grown-ups' example: 'Davidson can't possibly be the right man for the job: you know how bad his golf game is.'

How to fight back: 'What has that got to do with it? What's really relevant here?'

Slippery slope

What does it entail? A series of exaggerated steps leading to an overly extreme conclusion.

Playground example: 'You shouldn't tell your mum what you did. If you do, she might be really cross and never let you come out again and then all you'll be able to do is stay at home and you'll die of boredom!'

Grown-ups' example: 'If we accept the right of Mr Tomas to stay in Britain, then there's bound to be a surge of similar applications from around the world, the country will be overrun and we'll all be out of our jobs.'

How to fight back: 'How likely is that in reality? What other possible consequences might there be?'

What else? (restricting the options)

What does it entail? Presenting someone with a limited set of options, so that the one you want them to pick is clearly the strongest.

Playground example (sadly): 'Shoplifting's just a bit of fun – it's a laugh! What else have you got to do today, anyway – sit at home watching TV all afternoon?'

Grown-ups' example: 'Better let us install a completely new boiler, love, if you don't want to be freezing your socks off all winter.'

How to fight back: 'Are there any other alternatives? Might they be better?'

Mistaken link (post hoc/confusing cause and correlation)

What does it entail: Assuming that because something happened after or at the same time as something else, then the two events must be linked.

Playground example: 'I'm so glad I bought these trainers. I'd never have won the race otherwise. You should get a pair too!'

Grown-ups' example: 'The screen returned to normal shortly after I hit it. That's the way to deal with these things.'

How to fight back: 'Might this be a coincidence? What else could explain the events?'

Generalisation

What does it entail: Sweeping statements that are based on limited evidence.

Playground example: 'Tommy was mean to me today. All boys are horrid.'

Grown-ups' example: 'Our team has a centre forward who grew up in Brazil. He must be good.'

How to fight back: 'Are we accurately representing the wider situation?'

Everyone's doing it (universal claims)

What does it entail? Suggesting that something is much more widely accepted than it really is.

Playground example: 'Oh, come on – everyone knows that smoking's cool.'

Grown-ups' example: 'Anyone with any intelligence accepts that nuclear power is an impossibly dangerous option.'

How to fight back: 'Do they? Who is "everyone"? Where's the proof?'

▄■ It's not enough! (confusing necessary and sufficient conditions)

What does it entail? Assuming that just because something is *necessary* to achieve a particular outcome, it is *enough* on its own to guarantee this.

Playground example: 'My teacher told me I had to revise to pass the exam. I did revise, so how come I didn't pass?'

Grown-ups' example: 'I don't understand it. They said that if I bought the exercise machine, I'd lose two stone in three months. What went wrong?'

How to fight back: 'Might there be other factors that could play a part? What could they be?'

For the deeper thinker

 With older children who show a particular interest in this sort of thinking, you could try inventing short arguments together that illustrate a particular fallacy. Alternatively, you could take it in turns to guess each other's error. The sort of arguments that children invent are often surprisingly perceptive – not to mention funny.

ADVERT ALERT!

Adverts are a great place to start when learning to be media-aware, as their short length and obvious catchiness make them likely to appeal to children. It's very important to teach children to have a healthy attitude towards adverts: on the one hand, we need and benefit from some of the products they are describing; on the other, we'd be gullible, not to mention bankrupt, if we believed everything we were told.

When the adverts next come on the TV, instead of groaning and turning over, use this opportunity to try the following 'critical thinking' activities:

- **Rate the ad!** How many marks out of ten would you give that advert, just on gut instinct, without thinking about it too deeply? Why?

- **Mind-reading.** Ask your child if they think they might be able to read the mind of the advertiser and work out what they were trying to make the viewer believe. Get them to listen out for claims that are stated openly. These are the ones that are more likely to be true, as advertisers would get into trouble if they lied. However, even these promises should be considered carefully, as sometimes they can be interpreted in several different ways. More interesting, perhaps, are those hidden claims that are only implied. Praise your child if they spot any of the latter 'secret messages' (e.g. that wearing a particular perfume will make you more attractive, that eating a certain product will mean you'll be surrounded by happy smiling friends, or that using a particular cleaner will transform your bathroom into a perfect spotless representation of the one on TV). What do they think of these claims? Which do they believe? Which do they think are unlikely?

- **On trial.** Get your child to imagine they have the opportunity to interrogate the creator of the advert in an imaginary trial situation. What three questions would they like to ask to help them make up their mind about the product? For instance, if vague statistics were offered, such as 'nine out of ten dog owners say their dogs like this brand best', your child might want to know how many people were actually asked. How did they judge which brand their pet preferred? What were the alternatives? How much more expensive is this brand?

PRODUCT PACKAGING

Supermarket trips are a great opportunity to teach your child to be clued-up when it comes to advertising tricks. Every now and then, pick just one of the ideas below and get your kids to look out for:

- **Celebrities.** For example, well-known sports figures are used to represent healthy eating or actors for beauty products: these are 'you could be like this too' dreams to appeal to the insecure. How many can your child spot? Why do they think each celebrity was chosen for that product?

- **The tempting description.** From products that promise a healthier heart or a thinner waist to those that simply offer a truly delicious taste sensation, who can find the most outrageous example? Hair products are a good place to start ...

- **Ingredients.** Sometimes we're led to assume from its name or the picture on the packaging that a food product contains a particular ingredient such as fruit or chocolate, when a quick glance at the ingredients will soon reveal the terrible truth. Bonus marks for any examples of these that your child finds.

- **The pictures.** Often the image on the packaging of a product will contain pictures of products not included in the box. Give your children a basket each and see who can be first to find ten of these.

- **The small print.** For older children, can anyone find an example of a product that seems to promise something wonderful and then admits, in the smallest of small print, that there might be a slight catch? 'If used as part of a calorie-controlled diet' is the classic.

- **Freebies.** Are there any give-aways today? If there's something inside, how much does your child think it's really worth? What about tokens? How many need to be collected, and in what period of time? Good idea or bad, on balance?

- **Brand names.** Encourage your child to conduct an experiment. Can they find two equivalent products, one that is a well-known brand and one that is the supermarket's own? If you're happy to buy both, they could take them home and do a blind test using different members of the family. Which, on balance, was preferred? If the more expensive option was better, was it worth the extra money?

- **Positioning.** Lower shelves are often chosen for kids' products, so teach your children to be a step ahead when it comes to being shopping-savvy. They may genuinely want something and that's fine – but they should be aware that the shop has placed the product there specifically to tempt them.

For older children, you could set a combined challenge – who can find the product that uses the most hidden methods of persuasion?

Remember: there's no black or white here – you're not trying to be a kill-joy. Using these advertising tricks doesn't automatically mean that a product should be avoided. But your kids should grow up knowing that it's their decision to make: they're the ones in control, not the advertisers.

INTERNET ALERT

The Internet is an extraordinary research tool and it's great fun to try out new sites and see what's out there. Spend time online with your children when they're young, getting to know the sites they like. That way, you can explore together and talk through the issues that arise. As they get older, they're less likely to want you to join in, but by then you'll have helped them develop some in-built defences.

It can be a good idea to get your kids to work out a list of Internet-safe rules for themselves, listing the sort of information they can and can't give out and what to do if they come across anything worrying. It's much better if it comes from them, so trusting them with this responsibility can pay off, even if you need to make a few additions and alterations to what they come up with.

Teach your child that information found on the Internet is by no means always reliable. Encourage them, from an early age, to see themselves as investigators – looking for clues about a website before they accept what it says. Questions they might ask themselves could include the following:

- Who created the website?
- What is its purpose? Is it for information only, or is it trying to sell something?

- Does it carry any official logos?
- Is it neutral, or might it have any reason to be biased?
- If it contains information, does it show where this has come from?
- Is it asking me for information about myself? If so, does it really need this?

ON THE TRAIL OF . . .

Children absolutely love investigating all those 'mysteries' that we, as adults, so often hold fixed and far from romantic views about. Instead of taking the adventure out of the world, use these seemingly extraordinary events, sightings and stories to develop some critical thinking in practice. You could have, for example, a Loch Ness Monster afternoon. Or how about a Yeti hunt or a UFO Watch? With older children, the paranormal offers a wealth of topics – a quick hunt on the Internet will reveal a list of beliefs and hypotheses just crying out for some healthy scepticism. Once you've chosen your topic, the hunt is on! The challenge is to find a spread of evidence (photographs, findings, anecdotes, scientific reports, etc.) that represents different opinions.

If your child has an investigation journal (see Chapter 5), this could be a great place to record their discoveries. Alternatively, give them a huge sheet of paper and get them to create a massive collage – sorting the evidence in some way to reflect how credible they feel it is. Remember: the object is not that your child comes to hold the same opinion as you, but that he or she learns to assess the evidence, to consider the opposing sides and to reach a final verdict of their own.

Faced with the choice between changing one's mind, and proving that there is no need to do so, almost everybody gets busy on the proof.

John Kenneth Galbraith (1908–2006), economist

12 HOW TO THINK FLEXIBLY

Children very often seem to think that changing their mind is a sign of intellectual weakness rather than strength. Again, this probably comes from watching adults. Unfortunately, too often adults will either stick unwaveringly to their point of view when interacting with children, or they'll capitulate under the pressure of pleading. Both experiences confirm to a child that the strong hold firm and the weak give in – neither teaches the importance of being open to or forming quality reasoning.

It's important that children learn to make up their mind very carefully – to check the evidence, take other opinions into account, come up with lots of possibilities and avoid jumping to conclusions. Chapter 13 contains plenty of practical ideas for helping children to reach good decisions. However, it's arguably equally important to teach your child to *un-make* his or her mind as well. And this is easier said than done. It takes a particular combination of humility and self-confidence to be able to change one's mind when new facts turn up, when someone puts forward a stronger line of reasoning, or when you realise you've simply made a mistake.

Teaching our children to develop this sort of openness means they'll be much more likely not just to cope with, but to thrive on, change. Heather Dawson, author of the guide 'Faster faster', identifies the ability to tolerate ambiguity and uncertainty as one of the five qualities of a successful senior executive. In today's unpredictable climate, a readiness to shift positions in response to new information or events is becoming ever more important.

Flexibility is also a lynchpin for creativity: being able to look at things from a different angle, think about how to adapt and improve existing ideas and keep an open mind is far more valuable than grabbing one good idea and sticking with it, no matter what.

Possibly most importantly of all, it's the ability to think flexibly that lies at the heart of tolerance – and, although the main focus of this book is on characteristics and skills rather than values, this is clearly one value that we all, as parents and teachers, are likely to place pretty high up on our wish-list of qualities that we hope our children will develop.

The essayist and philosopher Emile Chartier summed this all up perfectly when he said: *'Nothing is more dangerous than an idea when it is the only one we have'*. This chapter offers a few hints on how to grow an open mind.

Quick tips

✓ Being flexible comes down to the ability to look rationally at opposing reasons and ideas. As such, it's important to encourage a reasoning culture in your home. Be prepared to give reasons for your beliefs and decisions and expect the same from your child.

✓ Teach your child that changing their mind on the basis of sound evidence is a sign that they are a 'good thinker' - it's evidence of their ability to reason for themselves.

✓ **Look out for suitable situations where this can be modelled.** For instance, if your child has come up with an idea, respond with something like, 'You're going to need to persuade me to change my mind about that one. Give me a reason!' After each reason, look a little more convinced, before finally cracking and saying, 'OK, you've convinced me. That's a really good idea. I'm going to change my mind.'

✓ If you find yourself changing your mind about something in your own day-to-day life, talk openly about this process.

✓ When problems arise, for example at school, teach your child from an early age to practise their mind-reading skills. How good can they become at guessing what the other people involved in the situation might be thinking and feeling?

Activities and games

You could try …

ODD ONE OUT

This can be played in all sorts of contexts. One person begins by choosing any three or four objects – they could be plants in a garden, objects in a kitchen drawer, characters in a story, animals in a zoo, pictures in an art gallery – the possibilities are endless. Everyone takes it in turns to suggest which of the set could be the odd one out, supporting their idea with a clear reason. It can be useful to formalise this process by insisting that everyone uses the simple phrase: 'I think … is the odd one out because …'

Emphasise the importance of listening to each other, so that ideas aren't repeated. Offer specific praise by commenting when a particularly unusual, creative or interesting suggestion is put forward. The game continues until one person can't think of any more ideas.

This game helps to develop flexibility of thought and creativity, encouraging children to think beyond the first 'right' answer. It also teaches them to be more observant and to analyse information in different ways.

School link

'Odd one out' can be used to explore school subjects in a fun and non-threatening way. Play it as a game, selecting three people, objects or concepts from your child's current topic, for example three wives of Henry VIII or three materials in science.

THE PATCHWORK GAME

This fantastic activity, developed by educationalist Mike Fleetham (see **www.thinkingclassroom.co.uk**), really helps to promote flexible thinking. You will need 16 squares, each containing a picture (which could be cut from a magazine or printed from the computer) or a word. There may be a theme – such as pirates, space or dinosaurs, or even aspects and characters from a story book – or you may prefer to have a completely random selection of objects and words. You can even begin the game by asking your child to call out 16 different words, while you write them on plain squares of paper or sticky notes.

With younger children, introduce the game by picking out two of the squares and inviting your child to think of ways in which the items are similar. Praise them for coming up with several answers when you thought you'd picked two really hard ones; then pretend to be choosing another two that will definitely 'catch them out' this time. Children love rising to a challenge, especially when there's a chance they're going to beat the grown-ups.

And another thought!

 It's great to use this to encourage your child to remember and talk about a family outing or school trip. Which words come into their mind when they think back about their day out?

Once your child is confident with finding similarities, the main activity is then to find a way of arranging all 16 squares in a four-by-four grid. There are three levels of challenge:

- **Brain-warming.** Each square must be similar in some way to the cards on its left and right.
- **Brain-boosting.** Each square must link not only to those on its left and right but also with the squares above and below it.
- **Brain-expanding.** Each card must logically link with the eight surrounding cards that touch either at the side or the corner.

If two or more children are playing this, you may need to establish ground rules, such as taking it in turns to place a square while giving a logical reason for its position. Then just sit back and watch! Occasionally you might like to check how your child is thinking by saying something like, 'This looks amazing! Right, I must be able to catch you out somewhere ... How about these two? Surely you haven't thought of a link between these?' They'll love proving you wrong!

With older children, you could add an extra level of challenge. When you've heard their reasoning behind a particular link, ask them to assess it: is it a weak link, a medium link or a strong link? If it's weak, can they shift the patchwork (or shift their reasoning) so that it contains more strong links?

Finish by asking which was your child's favourite linking idea. Which was the most imaginative link? Which two cards were the hardest to link? The idea is that by the end of the activity they'll have changed their mind lots of times in order to find the best links.

School link

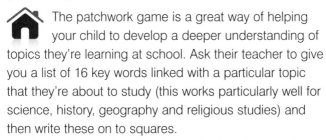 The patchwork game is a great way of helping your child to develop a deeper understanding of topics they're learning at school. Ask their teacher to give you a list of 16 key words linked with a particular topic that they're about to study (this works particularly well for science, history, geography and religious studies) and then write these on to squares.

Display the words somewhere clearly visible, such as tacked on to a wardrobe, mirror or fridge door. As your child learns more about the topic, they can arrange and rearrange the patchwork. It's a lovely chance for them to teach you about what they're learning as they explain the reasoning behind the shifts.

For the deeper thinker

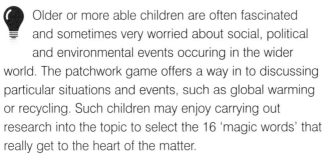 Older or more able children are often fascinated and sometimes very worried about social, political and environmental events occuring in the wider world. The patchwork game offers a way in to discussing particular situations and events, such as global warming or recycling. Such children may enjoy carrying out research into the topic to select the 16 'magic words' that really get to the heart of the matter.

IT'S A MYSTERY!

One person picks a series of mystery objects from around the house and places them in a bag or basket, covering them with a cloth. These are gradually unpacked by the others, who have to work out what sort of person owned the bag and what they were up to when they lost it. As each item emerges, the theories are obliged to change to incorporate the new clues – and the more creative, the better!

An alternative version of this is to turn it into a story-telling game. The first person takes out an object and starts to tell a story linked to it. The others take it in turns to offer a few more sentences as each new item is revealed. Praise any really inventive connections that you hear.

This game can of course be played without the basket. When you're next out walking somewhere, you and your child could take it in turns to spot interesting objects along the way. Together, you could invent a story that makes use of each of these objects. This is great fun for the naturally imaginative child, but it can also be really helpful for children who worry about having no ideas when it comes to writing stories at school.

PICTURE THIS!

This is a great activity to develop flexibility of thought and to help children learn that there are often lots of possible conclusions that can be drawn from a given set of evidence.

One person should think of an unusual starter event, such as the shops having entirely run out of chocolate bars, bright lights appearing in the sky last night, or a round patch of long grass appearing in the middle of the lawn. Then take it in turns to come up with as many possible reasons for this as you can.

And another thought!

This could be used to encourage your child to talk about any difficult situations they might be experiencing. For example, if they were disappointed to get a low score in a test after working really hard or if they feel that someone at school is behaving unkindly towards them, you could explore together all the possible explanatioins and causes. By including some really silly examples as well as a few more serious options, you can keep the atmosphere lighter.

THINK 'N' RUN

A great game to teach kids to keep an open mind until all the information is known, this activity requires a bit of preparation and creative thought on your part and needs a few children to take part.

Think of something that sounds wonderful to your kids – for example, they've just inherited their own desert island. How do the players feel? Get them to vote with their feet by assigning one side of the room or garden as 'happy' and the other as 'unhappy'. Then add a new piece of information. For example, the island is so remote that the 25-hour journey takes two planes and a boat to get there. How do they feel now? But ... the island comes with a private speedboat and personal jet. However ... it's not entirely private – there are residents who have the right to stay there as long as they want. But ... local custom dictates that all island dwellers give regular gifts to the island's owner! However ... the gifts are usually poisonous snakes ... You get the picture!

After each additional piece of information, the players must rethink their position and run to a position along the scale of happy to unhappy that represents their new state. Afterwards, it's worth asking them what they thought of the game. Can they invent their own versions?

WHAT ARE THEY THINKING?

With younger children, when you're looking at a picture book or a magazine together, if you come across a photograph or illustration that contains several people, use it to prompt a chat about the different things that they each might be thinking. What are they happy about? What might be making them feel worried? If they could each have one wish, what might it be? Add an extra challenge by taking turns with your child to choose a person in the

picture for each other to become. Then have a conversation together, pretending to be those people. This activity can become very imaginative and help your child to recognise that different people have different perspectives and ways of thinking.

SWITCH!

This game works well when you're out and about with your child, as it can be triggered by everyday things that you see around you.

One person starts by inviting the other to try to persuade them that something is true, for example that the battered Skoda on the corner is the best car ever, or that plastic carrier bags should be banned completely. The second person begins to do just this but must change sides and argue from the opposite point of view whenever the first person calls 'Switch!'

This game really tests your flexibility of thought, especially given that it's entirely up to the caller how often and how quickly they make you switch sides. It's best to keep each round relatively short – a minute works perfectly – so that the players can swap over fairly often and set each other new challenges. And be prepared to join in too – your children will love trying to catch you out!

THE BIG QUESTION IS . . .

A variation on the game above, this game is for three players and begins with one person – the question master

– setting a 'big question' for the other two to battle over. This question can be as deep or as dippy as you want – anything from 'The big question is … is there any such thing as magic?' to 'The big question is … is James Bond the best action hero?'; or, for the older, more fashion-conscious players, 'The big question is … should socks ever be worn with sandals?' The only rules are that there must be just two possible answers – either yes or no – and the answer should not be blindingly obvious.

The other two contestants must take up opposing positions. Then each puts forward one reason in defence of that viewpoint. Let's say it was the sandals question; one might argue 'The Romans wore socks with sandals and they brought us all sorts of vital things such as roads and hot baths', while the other might point out something equally philosophical such as 'Wearing socks on a hot day makes your feet smelly'.

The question master then chooses who to side with and the game begins. The contestant who isn't picked must then argue as persuasively as possible why their answer (either yes or no) is the right one, including as many reasons as they can. It's best to encourage them to take this slowly and to develop each point as fully and clearly as possible, otherwise they'll run out of ideas too quickly. Now, it's very important that the person who set the question listens carefully, as the moment they feel they've been convinced by the other side, they call out 'Jump!' It's then up to the other player to develop their own side of the argument in order to try to win the question master back. There can be any number of 'jumps' before the game ends, when both sides have run out of new arguments and counterarguments and the question master makes their final decision. Whoever they side with sets the next question.

This is a great game, as it really teaches the players that there's no stigma involved in changing your mind: the most important thing is to be constantly open to new ideas and arguments.

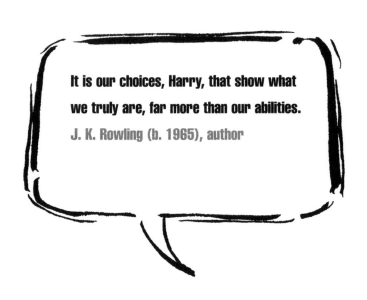

It is our choices, Harry, that show what we truly are, far more than our abilities.

J. K. Rowling (b. 1965), author

13 HOW TO MAKE WISE DECISIONS

We all know that making a guaranteed right decision can sometimes be impossible. But learning how to consider the various options, to weigh up the pros and the cons, and to anticipate potential consequences of specific courses of action certainly makes the process a lot more reliable.

Children today are making decisions all the time – some of which will have a serious impact on their lives. It's interesting to talk to them about how they do this. Perhaps because life seems to be getting ever faster these days – with immediate access to information, entertainment and communication – decisions also appear to be made worryingly quickly. Too often, our children rely on gut instinct and what others say to guide them. Thinking through the options must seem tiresomely slow.

That's why it's so important to begin building good decision-making habits from an early age. There are some serious issues at hand and, as parents or teachers, we can't rely on being there to help our children make good decisions all the time. Instead, we need to help them develop the inclination and the understanding to do this for themselves.

This chapter and the next two are deliberately placed towards the end of the book, as they deal with skills that require a combination of various qualities introduced so far. If our children are to learn to deal wisely with dilemmas, for instance, then it will involve creativity and an investigative spirit to come up with a range of options, risk-taking to pick a course of action, and persistence to follow it through.

This means that many of the activities described earlier

should help your child to become a skilful decision-maker.
This chapter offers a few more ideas to try.

 Quick tips

✓ Where appropriate, talk openly
about decisions that you are
making. Show that you are
considering the pros and the
cons of different options and,
if possible, get your child
involved as well. Choosing a
holiday, for instance, or
planning a celebration for
someone's birthday can be a
really interesting project in
which they can take part.

✓ Teach your child the value of
putting their difficult
decision to one side and either
'sleeping on it' or simply doing
something completely
different for a while. In his

fascinating book 'What's the Point of School?', Guy Claxton (2008) describes research that shows that allowing time for information to incubate in the back of the mind can sometimes be more helpful than the attempt to be explicit and methodical. We tend to underplay this aspect of our intelligence.

✓ Help your child learn that by thinking things through they are doing all that they can. If, after that, it turns out that the decision wasn't the right one, reassure them that you're not going to waste time worrying about what could have

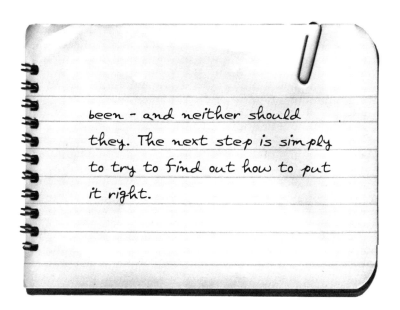

been – and neither should they. The next step is simply to try to find out how to put it right.

Activities and games

You could try ...

I'VE GOT A PROBLEM ...

The first step in making a good decision is to consider all your options. This game encourages children to do just that. One player thinks of a problem situation, which could be serious or silly – for example, you're stuck up a tree or you've fallen out with your best friend. Then you take it in turns to come up with as many possible solutions as you can.

At the end, each person should pick the idea they thought was the funniest, the one they thought was most original and the one that was the most sensible.

TRADING PLACES

It's a good idea to encourage your child to consider alternative viewpoints before making a decision. This very simple series of questions is worth remembering when discussing problem issues:

- How many different people might have an opinion about this?
- What might *x* think? Why?
- What might *y* think? Why?
- What do *you* think? Why?

IN THE BALANCE

A very visual way of helping younger children to understand how to think through a decision is to use a set of 'decision scales'. These can sit in your child's bedroom and be used whenever an interesting decision arises.

You will need a set of pan-balance scales (the type with a tray on each side of a central pivot), some plastic building bricks and some sticky notes. Introduce the idea that decision-making is rather like weighing: once you've come up with lots of possible options, you need to weigh up the good and the bad points of each one at a time.

Imagine you're helping your child to make a decision about what they'd like to do for their birthday. Together you could generate four or five possible options, and then narrow it down to two or three main contenders. Focus on one option from the short-list and ask your child to suggest its good points. Write each idea on a sticky label, attach it to a plastic brick and place it on one side of the scales. Repeat for the bad points. Which side is heavier? On balance, was the option a good or a bad idea?

Help your child to see that this is basically the same process that we use throughout our lives. Ask your child to help you use the scales to make a decision you're facing.

For the deeper thinker

 A great way of demonstrating that it's not always the number of pros and cons that matters, but their relative importance, is to use a variety of different-sized plastic bricks. As each point is raised, ask your child whether they think it's a more or a less important point – and use the appropriate-sized brick to represent it. It's worth linking this with the concept of risk-taking. Sometimes a few really important potential pluses may outweigh a lot of smaller minuses.

TUG OF WAR

A useful alternative to this for the older child is to see decision-making as a tug-of-war process. When considering a decision, encourage your child to write all their thoughts on individual sticky notes. They might like to ask their friends and different members of the family for ideas to include as well.

The resulting jumble of pros and cons can then be stuck on a tug-of-war line from 'good idea' at one end to 'bad idea' at the other. Which side do they think has the most strength?

JUST SUPPOSE . . .

It's great practice for your child to try out their decision-making skills in the context of some imaginary, hypothetical situations. Try to pick decisions that will really grab their attention and that you'd all find interesting to discuss together.

Here are a few examples:

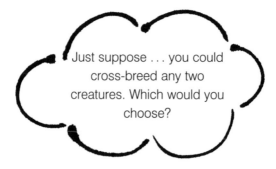

Just suppose . . . you could cross-breed any two creatures. Which would you choose?

Just suppose ... you could be told the answer to any one question. What would you ask?

Just suppose ... you could be any character from a story for a week. Who would you be?

Just suppose ... you were stuck on a desert island. What one item would you choose to have with you?

Just suppose ... you could invent one new law for the country. What would it be?

Each time, begin by brainstorming loads of possible ideas, then whittle these down to the final winning idea by considering the pros, cons and consequences. This will help to teach your child that good decision-making takes time. The first option to enter one's head is not necessarily going to be the best. It's worth sticking with it a bit longer.

REVERSE THINKING

A creative thinking tool sometimes used by businesses, reverse thinking involves asking the opposite question to the one that is being considered. This can act as a prompt for all sorts of unexpected ideas. It works very well with children as a way of helping spark genuine options that they may not have thought of otherwise.

For instance, if your child is trying to decide how to approach their next football match or how to spend their pocket money, you might ask 'What's the best way to lose at football?' or 'What's the best way to waste all your pocket money?' Children tend to find this really funny, and they enjoy thinking through the options much more than if the question were the 'right' way round. By clarifying the opposite situation, it is surprising how often the activity sparks off some genuinely useful ideas.

And another thought!

 This can be a very good way of getting your child to focus on something that may be a particular issue for them but that tends to lead to arguments or distress when approached more conventionally. For example, 'What's the best way to . . . be late for school/fail an exam/ruin a friendship/get run over?'

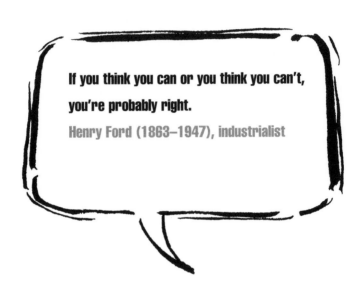

If you think you can or you think you can't, you're probably right.

Henry Ford (1863–1947), industrialist

14 HOW TO ENJOY SOLVING PROBLEMS!

We all wish we could do more to help when our children are worrying about a problem they've got to face. This seems to affect some children more than others, but it's going to be the case that every child, at some point or another, gets themselves tied up in knots over something – however small it may seem to us.

One way to deal with this is to step in and sort it all out for them. It's so tempting, especially when the solution seems quite clear to us and we know we can do something about it. But diving in and playing super-mum or super-dad isn't always the best course of action. For one thing, it leaves us with the dilemma of knowing when to stop. And for another, it's not helping our kids to build up their own set of problem-solving skills.

Imagine we could turn the whole situation upside-down. Forgive me for sounding gimmicky for a moment, but what if we taught our children, from as early an age as possible, to replace the word 'problem' with 'challenge'? Tricky to introduce if your kids are older – they're likely to look at you as though you've well and truly lost it! But if we adopted this approach from day one, that's got to make a real difference to the way they look at life.

Of course, it would have to be backed up with action. Instead of hiding our problems from our kids, or looking stressed, getting angry or even leaping around in a frenzy, what if they saw us smiling (wryly will do), rolling up our sleeves and settling down to do some serious thinking, at least some of the times when we're facing challenges of our own? What if they heard us talking through the different options, weighing them up and working out how best to move forward?

The title quote for this chapter just can't be beaten: *'If you think you can or you think you can't, you're probably right.'* Imagine growing up with that sort of proactive mindset, knowing that tricky situations are bound to come along – and that they affect all of us – but that it's nearly always possible, with a bit of ingenuity and positive thinking, to find a solution. The answer is out there somewhere. It exists. It just needs finding! How different would that child be from the one who was told not to worry when something went wrong, that mum or a teacher or someone – *anyone* but the child – would sort it all out for them?

One of the underlying themes of this book is that children need to be prepared if they're not only to cope with, but also to thrive in, a very different future. This chapter describes one of the most important skills they can develop. If we can help our kids to enjoy solving problems – to know that they've got what it takes to find that creative solution – then what a great attitude that would be to take with them into the adult world.

What's more, by teaching your child to be willing to rise to the challenge of solving problems, then you increase the control they feel over events in their own life. That's not to say that every problem will be solved – but there are often more things than we realise that are within our control. And at least once they've done the thinking, they can sit back and let go of the stress.

Quick tips

✓ When your child has a problem, don't leap in with an answer. Try to give them space to work things out for themselves. But help by all means - by listening, sympathising if necessary, perhaps sometimes by repeating and clarifying what they're saying, maybe asking occasional questions or prompting them to consider alternative solutions. Show you understand their worries and feelings.

✓ Encourage your child to believe that, nine times out of ten, they will be able to find a solution if they put the effort in. Prompt their thinking by asking questions such as:

- That sounds like a really tricky situation. Can you think of any way around this one?

- Wow - that really is a challenge! But I bet if anyone can sort it out, you can. You're great at solving problems!

- Why not start by coming up with as many possible solutions as you can - it doesn't matter how silly they sound - and then we could think through them together and see if you can spot the winner?

✓ **Teach your child to take responsibility for situations that arise.** Teach them to work out how they came about, to accept their own role if they had a part in them and to set about considering all the different possible solutions that they can think of. Link it to being creative - it makes it much more fun! For example, recently we were trying to work out why anyone might have draped the school toilets with vast quantities of toilet roll; the girls who were helping gleefully said 'It's a creative thinking game!' and promptly began to come up with explanations. It's a mindset – and one that you have a real chance to influence.

✓ Encourage your child to consider the problem from different points of view. Don't immediately take their side – no matter how trustworthy and honest your child is, he or she is also young, inexperienced in viewing all sides fairly, and highly likely not to be impartial.

✓ Show your child that you trust and value their problem-solving skills by asking their advice – where appropriate – when you are facing a problem of your own.

Activities and games

You could try ...

THINKING FRIENDS

One really great way of helping young children to begin solving their own problems is to introduce them to a 'thinking friend'.

This can be a really fun activity to do together. Start by inviting your child to select a few suitable toys whose 'personalities' seem to fit with particular thinking talents. Keep this simple – your child might, for instance, pick three toys, one for each of the thinking talents below:

- asking interesting questions;
- coming up with lots of creative ideas;
- making wise decisions.

This is best illustrated with an example. Imagine your child has found three toys. You've got a toy cat, for instance, who's always getting herself into trouble because of her unremitting curiosity – she just can't stop asking questions and trying to find their answers. Then there's a squirrel puppet, who is very creative and can be relied upon to come up with ten ideas for every situation or challenge that arises. And finally, there's that old tatty elephant, the one who's falling apart at the seams but who is so wise that all the other toys come to him whenever a sensible decision needs to be made.

You get the idea (and your child will do far better than I have!).

Next time a particular problem situation arises – for example, your child needs to work out what to do about a tricky friendship issue at school – you can line up the relevant toy or toys and turn to them for help. You might get your child to imagine what sort of questions the cat would like to ask about the situation. Once you've used this tactic to build a clearer picture of the facts, then it might be time to involve the squirrel. How many different possible solutions can she come up with? Emphasise that it doesn't matter how crazy they are. The great thing about the creative stage of the thinking process is that children feel liberated by not having to second-guess what will be considered a sensible solution and what might sound silly.

Next, what would happen if we took two or three of these options to the elephant? What do you think he might say were their good points? What might he think wasn't so good about them?

And, of course, you don't need to involve all three toys. I'm doing this mostly to help illustrate how the process works, whereas in reality this might get too complicated. But the point of it, I hope, is becoming clear. By providing a one-step-removed way of tackling a situation, we create a less threatening environment in which to discuss what might otherwise be quite delicate problems. It's somehow much easier for a child to be asked to consider what someone else might be thinking about a situation than to reveal their own thoughts. And it's also more fun!

This may sound a bit bizarre, but believe me, it works! I have seen a class of five- and six-year-olds engage in surprisingly advanced discussions after having been drawn into these debates by a soft toy whom we named 'Brains'. Brains, they accepted with earnest faces and total conviction, was a very good thinker who was able to provide all sorts of interesting ideas and suggestions that might help them.

There are several variations on this activity. If your child's not one for soft toys – or if they've a particularly vivid imagination – they might prefer to dream up and draw a separate magical creature for each thinking talent. They could give them suitable names and you could have fun making up some stories together that show them putting their super-skills into practice.

THE GREAT PROBLEM-SOLVING MACHINE

Another option that's great for practical, hands-on kids is to create a special mechanical device to help them overcome tricky challenges. Start by having a chat together about what stages are involved when tackling a problem.

Depending on the age and enthusiasm of your child, he or she might – with a little prompting – realise that their machine needs, for example, to have sections for (i) checking the facts; (ii) considering what other people might say about the situation; (iii) generating lots of solutions; (iv) looking for the good points of an idea; (v) looking for its bad points; and (vi) choosing the best way forward.

The next step is to supply as many junk modelling bits and pieces as you can lay your hands on and then help your child to create a Heath Robinson-style wacky machine – with labels for each stage of the process.

Of course, the success of each of these approaches depends on how much and how skilfully you use these thinking props. It will be up to you to judge when an occasion might be helped by calling on the appropriate 'friend' and asking your child to try a bit of mind-reading and guess what that character is thinking. You certainly don't need to feel this has to be done every time. But, as a method for helping children to think things through for themselves, it's definitely worth having up your sleeve.

THE PROBLEM-SOLVING PLAN

Why not make a 'Our Family's Problem-Solving Plan' poster to put up somewhere in your home? Your child could help you by typing it up and illustrating it. Steps could be something like this:

1   **Think aloud.** Who can I talk to about this?

2   **Collect the facts.** What do I know about the situation? Is there anything else I need to find out?

3   **Check that the problem really is a problem.** Might I be jumping to conclusions? Could there be another explanation for the facts?

3   **Gather ideas.** How many opinions and possible solutions can I think of? How many can I find out from other people?

4   **Pick a course of action.** Weighing up the pros and the cons, which is the best plan to choose? If it's a bit daunting and is likely to take some time, try breaking it up into smaller steps.

5 **If possible, give it a little time to 'sit' in the mind.** Might I change my mind if I sleep on it? How do I feel an hour, a day or two later (depending on urgency, of course)?

6 **Don't waste time.** If it's the right thing to do, it's time to go for it! Having a strop, panicking or watching TV won't help.

Help your child to recognise that they've done the best they can – they've acted in a logical way and have given time and effort to finding the best way forward. If the solution doesn't work, at least it was the best one they had. There will always be other factors outside of their control that may get in the way – they shouldn't be ashamed if it goes wrong.

CTB: CREATIVE THINKING BACKWARDS

If you're helping your child to work through a problem situation, once you've both got all the facts at your fingertips then it's time to do a bit of 'creative thinking backwards'.

Are there any other explanations for the situation – is the problem really a problem? I've used these questions with eight- and nine-year olds, as a chance to explore the sort of conclusions young children are prone to jumping to (for example, 'My best friend isn't talking to me – it must be because she hates me', 'I saw a shadow in the corner – it must have been a ghost!', 'I've scored badly in the test – it's because I'm rubbish at maths').

One approach is to give your child a big sheet of paper with their problem written in the middle. Encourage them to think of as many explanations for this situation as they can – not just the one they immediately assumed was true. Taking the examples above, children come up with all sorts of ideas, such as 'My best friend might be worrying or thinking about something else', 'What I saw was probably just the curtain moving' and 'My test score might have been low because I never understood fractions and didn't ask my teacher to help me'. The great thing is that it seems to take remarkably little practice to develop this mindset. All you have to say are the trigger words, 'What other explanations might there be?', and you'll get a whole list of possibilities. Of course this activity can be done verbally too and is very useful at bedtime (as is the one below), if you've a child who tends to worry about things before they fall asleep.

CTF: CREATIVE THINKING FORWARDS

If there really are no plausible alternative explanations and the problem really is a problem, then next comes the 'creative thinking forwards' part: how many different possible courses of action are there? What could your child do to make the situation better? What could your child suggest others do? If necessary, what could you do?

This stage should be completely free of judgement: all ideas, even the silly ones, should be included. Including these has the benefit of lightening the exercise and the mood – and perhaps generating an idea that might act as a stepping stone to something more plausible.

Consider similar problems faced before – how did you tackle them? Is there anything that can be learned from past experiences?

SAVED THE DAY!

Make it a family tradition that you praise your kids whenever they 'save the day' by doing something ingenious. For example, you've forgotten your keys, so how are you going to get into the house? The table's wobbly, so what should we do about it? The bolt's stuck and there's someone panicking in the bathroom! How can we get them out?

You get the idea. Basically, whenever you find yourself momentarily stumped by one of those day-to-day crises that affect us all, instead of making a quick decision yourself, be prepared to give it a bit more time and involve your kids. It gives them a real sense of importance within the family and builds their own belief in themselves as problem-solvers. They'll also love keeping a tally of who's saved the day the most times.

YOUR CHALLENGE IS TO . . .

This is a quick game that can be played anywhere and that is always good fun. Take it in turns to set each other entirely outrageous challenges. How do you build an igloo in a desert? How can you kidnap an elephant in broad daylight? How might you escape from an underwater cave when you've got no diving equipment? (Your child will be able to come up with many more!) The task is then to come up with a five-step plan to achieve the impossible.

MYSTERY ROUTES

Next time you've got to go to the supermarket, set your child a real-life problem – their task is to choose which route you're going to take. Let them use a map and pick whichever route they'd like, and then direct you all the way there ... No sat nav allowed!!

MOVE THE MOUNTAIN!

Based on an ancient Indian legend and on the puzzle invented by French mathematician Edouard Lucas in 1883, this brain teaser is a wonderful activity to develop problem-solving skills. You need a number of objects of different sizes that will balance on top of each other. Books work well for this – but it's also great fun with cushions if you've got more space. Place them in a pile in order of size, with the largest at the bottom and the smallest on top. With beginners, try this initially with four objects – then move up to six or eight with those children who really take to the puzzle.

Mark out three spaces as shown in the picture and position the pile in the left-hand space.

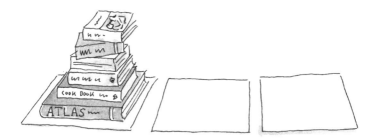

The task is simply to move the 'mountain' into the space on the right-hand side. The rules are as follows:

- Move only one object at a time.
- Only an object on top of a pile can be moved – no slipping objects out from the middle!
- Objects can be moved into an empty space or placed on top of a larger object. An object must not be placed on top of one that is smaller in size.

This activity provides a good opportunity to model to your child the value of persistence. It's easy to get frustrated and give up – so try to create a fun atmosphere, perhaps where you take it in turns to move the objects. You could say things like 'I'm not going to give up with this!' or 'Think of how great we'll feel if we manage this!' so your child sees you finding the task challenging too.

And another thought!

A wooden version of this game, *Pagoda Challenge*, by Square Root Games, can be purchased from good toy outlets.

TIED UP IN KNOTS!

This game is a really fun way of introducing the sort of sequential thinking that helps with problem-solving. You need quite a bit of space and a group of five or six people – probably not including adults, unless you're particularly bendy!

One person should stand back. The others hold hands in a circle and then proceed to tie themselves in knots, by twisting and turning and interweaving under arms. The only rule is that no one should let go of another person's hands. They can use their legs to loop over arms as well, if you feel this is safe. At the end, the 'watcher' should try to untie them by working out the right order in which to undo the tangle.

FLOW DIAGRAMS

A simple but effective strategy for generating and visualising the series of logical steps required to solve a problem is to use a flow diagram. The great thing about this strategy is that children can learn to scribble one of these on any scrap of paper, with as few or as many boxes as they wish. The boxes can be any shape or size, with arrows between them to show their order. They can contain words, pictures or both – it depends on your child.

We often take for granted our planning skills, but children of all ages tend to find this really challenging. Get your child to draw a flow diagram of preparations for a real-life event, such as a birthday party or a holiday. Setting the activity within a genuinely meaningful context like this will help your child to see the value of the technique – and it has the advantage of seeming less like a school lesson.

For the deeper thinker

 Try making this activity more challenging by applying it to something more abstract; for instance, can your child draw a flow chart to show how to become a genius or how to make the world a better place? If your child is particularly artistic, their diagram could be illustrated and turned into a poster to put on the wall.

THE NEWSPAPER PROBLEM

This exercise was suggested in Roger von Oech's (1998) book *A Whack on the Side of the Head* and can be used only once, but it's a great activity to introduce some important 'rules' for solving problems. Get a piece of newspaper and lay it out flat on the ground. Here's the challenge: can your child(ren) find a way of arranging the sheet so that when two people are standing on it, facing each other, they are not able to touch one another?

When I've done this with older children, they've really enjoyed coming up with all sorts of solutions. The secret of this activity is to use their attempts to point out three things:

- **The importance of breaking rules.** If your child asks something like 'Can I tear up the paper/replace it with a bigger sheet/stand holding a rope and lean backwards/keep just part of my feet on the paper', tell them what a fantastic idea that is and praise them for challenging the rules. Explain that, in many situations, one of the obstacles to finding a solution is that we too readily accept that things just have to be the way they are – and you're really impressed that they're not making that mistake. Then tell them that in fact, for this game, they can't do any of these things! In my experience, this always makes them laugh and increases the sense of challenge.

- **The importance of thinking flexibly.** Encourage your child to try out everything – no idea can ever be too silly. Most will be absolutely rubbish and that's completely fine – as there may be the occasional gem hidden among them.

- **The importance of being logical.** Part way through the activity, encourage your children to try to think logically: what is the problem with their situation? This should get them to stop and consider how they could prevent their bodies from touching. They might initially think of tying up their hands (though of course they could still touch other parts of the body), then they should eventually realise that they need something between them. I've seen A-level students try all sorts of possibilities at this stage (flip board, coats, chairs) with hilarious results, until one bright spark suddenly has a flash of inspiration: the door! The sense of satisfaction is enormous, but it's the learning that has taken place during the activity that really makes it worthwhile.

FLYING MACHINES

Another version of the activity above, now the challenge is to make a device out of paper that will travel the furthest across the room. What is great fun about this game is that children will spend hours putting together the most complex paper aeroplanes conceivable, having jumped to the conclusion that a device that flies must be a plane.

At the end, hold a contest to see which device wins. As with 'The newspaper problem', praise your child for the problem-solving tricks that were demonstrated: a willingness to (i) 'break the rules' (e.g. cut the paper in half to make it lighter); (ii) think flexibly (count the number of 'failed' attempts and praise your child for their abundance of ideas); and (iii) be logical (comment when your child has been methodical in their planning, measuring and so on).

Then – if none of your kids have beaten you to it – stun them all with how far your device (a simple scrunched-up ball of paper) can travel. Ask them why they didn't think of this, and use the activity to highlight the importance of thinking laterally.

REAL-LIFE LATERAL THINKING

Many books have been written on the topic of creative thinking. A best-selling favourite is *A Whack on the Side of the Head* (von Oech, 1998), which describes all sorts of real-life problem-solving situations that have been solved by using the sort of approaches described above (and many more). *The Mechanism of Mind* (De Bono, 1969) also explores several examples of creative thinking. Here are two wonderful examples that you could challenge your children to think about:

- **Waiting for the lift (De Bono).** A new high-rise building in Chicago began to face problems as more and more of the offices were taken up by companies. Too many people were trying to use the lifts at rush-hour in the morning and evening. This led to lots of complaints about waiting for ages for the lift. Imagine you were in charge of finding a solution. What would you do?

- **Litter trouble (von Oech).** Some time ago, a city in Holland found itself with a serious litter problem. One area in particular was becoming a real mess, with cigarette butts, bottles, newspapers and other rubbish scattered regularly. Imagine you were advising. How many solutions can you think of?

In each case, encourage your kids to generate as many ideas as possible, before choosing their final, best idea. Afterwards, you could reveal what really happened.

When I've tried the first example with children, their suggestions have ranged from the wacky (jet packs and a fireman's pole) to the practical (high-speed lifts between popular floors, staggered starting and finishing times for the companies that shared the building) to the seriously lateral (get rid of the lifts entirely and introduce exercise classes and incentives to help people cope with the stairs). In reality, the story goes that one female manager turned the question around, asking 'How can I make the wait less boring?' rather than 'How can I move people more quickly?' The solution was floor-to-ceiling mirrors in the lobby!

In the case of the litter problem, the city tried doubling the fine for dropping rubbish, and then increasing the number of people patrolling the area – both with little effect. The lateral leap came when someone suggested developing bins that paid people to put litter in them. Rather than dismissing this as an impossible idea from a financial point of view, this led to a discussion about how else people could be rewarded for being tidy. The solution? Bins that sensed when something had been put inside them and then played a recorded joke (which changed every fortnight)!

PRACTICAL PROBLEM-SOLVING

If you're short of something to do one day, why not set your kids a practical problem-solving challenge? For instance:

- Make a device to protect an egg when it's dropped from a second-floor window.
- Build the highest tower made only of newspaper and plastic cups.
- Create something that will transport – with as much precision as possible – a tennis ball from a ground-floor window to a particular point outside.
- Design a contraption to help a hard-boiled egg to float in the bath.
- Construct a bridge across the garden path, made entirely of spaghetti (in its dried state!) and marshmallows. Devise a way to test its strength.

The great thing about this is that children will engage willingly in really complex thinking without perceiving it as 'work'. Remember that making time for a chat afterwards is what really adds value to this sort of activity. How did your children go about this task? How many possible ideas did they try? What proved most tricky about the challenge? How did they overcome this? If they didn't manage it, have they any ideas for things they could try next time?

RANDOM-INPUT PROBLEM-SOLVING

This little trick is definitely worth teaching your kids. When your mind has gone blank and you're really stuck for an idea or solution, one method that can have surprisingly interesting results is the random-input method. Simply open a magazine or newspaper randomly and point to a word on the page. Repeat two or three times so you have a few options. Then let your mind mull over how any or all of these words might provide the key to the solution to your problem.

Sometimes our mind simply needs a trigger to jump-start it again. Random words can lead to all sorts of innovative ideas that you'd never have thought of without them.

COMPUTER GAMES

There are some excellent games out there that can play a part in developing creative thinking and problem-solving skills (not to mention persistence, concentration and coping with set-backs, as I mentioned earlier). As part of a varied life, they're not to be ruled out.

Avoid games with violent content – there's simply no need to get these when there are other such wonderful options to try instead.

Take the time to learn and play them yourself – join in with your child and share the experiences. You'll learn a lot about each other.

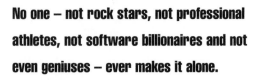

No one – not rock stars, not professional athletes, not software billionaires and not even geniuses – ever makes it alone.

Malcolm Gladwell (b. 1963), author and cultural commentator

15 HOW TO HAVE SOCIAL SAVVY

Referring to research conducted a few years ago by the sociologist Annette Lareau, Malcolm Gladwell, in his book, *Outliers: The Story of Success*, points out that certain children are brought up in a way that gives them enormous advantages both while they are growing up and later in life.

The secret? Social savvy. A vital ingredient if we're to raise children who will make the most of their abilities and achieve their full potential.

It hinges on a parent's ability to teach their child, from an early age, to interact comfortably in adult settings. We need to learn how to raise children who know that they have a valued place within society, that they are worthy of adult attention and interest, and that they have the right to speak up whenever they need certain information or require circumstances to be adapted in order to allow them to progress.

Gladwell links this with the psychologist Robert Sternberg's work on practical intelligence. Sometimes called 'street smarts', it's all about 'knowing what you need to get from a given situation and how best to go about getting it'.

And it makes sense. In almost any field, if you look at the people who are most successful, you'll find individuals who have – and have always had – an inner confidence in their own worth. That doesn't automatically imply arrogance, and it needn't mean they lack humility. It's simply that they have a sense of entitlement, of fitting in. What's more, this isn't just something that's valuable for aspiring leaders: life runs a whole lot more smoothly for anyone if they've developed these sorts of skills.

Gladwell argues that this 'secret of success' comprises *'a set of skills that have to be learned. [Social savvy] has to come from somewhere, and the place where we seem to get these kinds of attitudes and skills is from our families.'*

What makes this so important is the fact that, particularly in today's world, none of us can achieve independently. We need each other. As Howard Gardner (2006), founder of Multiple Intelligence Theory, explains, *'[These days] many people work on problems which cut across disciplines … They converge on a geographical area, work together in teams, build on one another's knowledge, then separate and maybe connect electronically, but maybe never work together again.'* By building on each others' suggestions, we open up the possibility of developing far more creative and innovative solutions than we would alone.

An important feature here is what Gardner calls 'inter-personal intelligence'. He describes this as being sensitive to other peoples' moods, feelings and temperaments, being able to cooperate within a group, and knowing how to bring out the best in the people we're dealing with.

Children get some experience of working in groups in primary school, though they're rarely taught about the different and valuable roles that we can each play – activities are more focused on developing listening and collaborative skills. This tends to get phased out as they move up through school: group work is likely to play little part in formal education, while exams still almost entirely emphasise solo achievement. While this is the case, schools will continue to fail to represent the reality of life situations.

A lot to think about! Let's get on with some practical tips.

Quick tips

✓ Help your child to learn that
no one can be good at
everything. Instead, a real
sign of intelligence is
recognising and valuing your
own strengths and knowing
where to go to 'fill in the
gaps'. Tell your child - often
and specifically - what you
like and admire about them.
Point out their wonderful
characteristics and skills.
And when obstacles or problem
situations arise, urge them to
be confident, friendly and
proactive in asking for what
they need, seeking advice and
sorting out a solution. (see
Chapter 14 for more ideas.)

✓ Talk things through with your children as a matter of course. Encourage them to discuss their ideas and feelings, to ask questions and to negotiate - within reason - ways forward that suit both you and them.

✓ Create opportunities for your children to interact with adults other than yourself. For instance, teach them to answer the door and to know how to respond, respectfully and appropriately, to whoever is there. When visiting the doctor or dentist, encourage your child to explain for him- or herself what it is that is wrong. And when you have friends over, expect your children to spend at least part of the time joining in with the discussions. Remember: your aim is to raise children who are comfortable, assured and friendly in the company of anyone and everyone.

✓ **Teach children about small talk.** This is not something that comes naturally to everyone, and so it's worth looking out together for topics that could be successful to use in a conversation with someone they don't know so well.

✓ First impressions are, as we all know, incredibly important.

Show older children how to make eye contact, and to smile and shake hands firmly with adults in appropriate situations such as interviews and formal gatherings.

✓ **Children sometimes feel less sure of themselves if they're not natural leaders, as this is the only team role that really stands out in school.** And yet, very few of us need to be leaders to live successful and happy lives. What is more important is that we find our own role within the group dynamic. Try to find opportunities for your children to engage in group challenges

and tasks, and make it a rule
that, each time they do so,
they try out a different
team role. It's great to teach
children that they can be
just as valued whatever their
role - whether they are the
person who generates creative
ideas, or the one who is
fantastically methodical and
well organised, or the one who
sees the problems and finds
ways around them.

✓ When your children are
engaged in creative activities,
especially where a degree of
collaboration is required, refer
often to the fact that good
creative thinkers will use each

others' ideas as building blocks. This represents a dramatic shift for many children - but one that, in my experience, they get used to quickly. In fact, it's one of the most rewarding changes that you see in children engaged in the sort of thinking approaches described in this book. The squabbling over competing ideas reduces as children learn to take pride in the way in which they incorporated someone else's suggestion into their own, resulting in a fantastic joint solution. 'I've a bendy brain!' is how some of the youngest children at our school describe this feeling.

Activities and games

You could try ...

INSPIRING QUOTES

Three great quotes to teach your kids:

'There are no ordinary people' – *C. S. Lewis*.

'As the ball and the parts it is made of
   Are bound and held fast at the seam –
   The strength of the team is the player;
   And the strength of the player the team' – *Rudyard Kipling*.

'Snowflakes are one of nature's most fragile things, but just look
   what they can do when they stick together' – *Vista M. Kelly*.

MY DAEMON

In Philip Pullman's classic novel for children, *Northern Lights*, humans have their own 'daemons' – magical animal companions that in some way represent each person's inner nature.

A good way of helping your child to think about their own characteristics and to consider how others might see them is to ask: 'If you had an animal daemon, what would it be?' After chatting about the reasons for their choice, ask your child whether other people (friends, teachers, siblings, people at clubs and other groups) would have guessed this. Would they have suggested other animals? If so, why might this be? This can help to uncover the fact that we often behave differently in different situations – we don't always reveal the same set of characteristics. This sort of self-awareness is useful: if we can learn more deliberately to bring out particular traits that will suit particular situations, then we're developing an important aspect of 'social savvy'.

PEBBLES IN A POND

Teach your child that our actions always have repercussions. It's like throwing a pebble into a pond – even a small stone causes ripples that radiate much further than you'd expect. Simple positive actions – like smiling at someone, thanking them, showing an interest in something that's on their mind, making them feel special in some way – can make a huge difference to how they feel and what they do. And people who have this sort of uplifting effect on others are likely to find their way through life much more smoothly.

ROLE PLAY

Younger children often love acting out different roles and, if guided a little, this can play a valuable part in helping them to learn how to articulate themselves in a variety of situations. Suggest a scenario – for example, get your children to imagine they are in a shop; they decide what to buy, pay for it and leave, only to realise that the change they've been given isn't quite right. What would they do?

The aim is to use this to teach your children to be direct, concise and polite in asking for what they want or explaining what they think and feel. It's also a great chance to learn about the value of creative thinking and compromise. You and they will be able to think of lots more scenes like this, which, as well as giving vent to their natural imagination, will help to teach them how to be assertive in the best possible way.

A fun way to introduce this can be to suggest that your children act out the scene initially by taking on the characters of celebrities or cartoon/television/book characters. For instance, how would Superman/Cruella Deville/Snow White/James Bond/Homer Simpson behave in this situation? This offers a light-hearted way in to some quite serious topics and helps to highlight the contrast between different possible (or impossible!) approaches.

PUBLIC SPEAKING

This should be something that your children learn at school. Nevertheless, support at home is always a great thing! Teach your child the following essential steps:

1 **Know your stuff.** Research the subject carefully beforehand.

2 **Know your audience.** Think about who you'll be speaking to and what they will find interesting.

3 **Be prepared.** Create a set of prompts (this often works well using flash cards) with key words and phrases to guide you through your talk.

4 **Practise.** Rehearse the talk lots of times and do so in the position you'll be adopting for the real thing. For instance, if it's a school assembly, encourage your child to stand up while practising their talk and get them to close their eyes briefly beforehand, imagining they are actually in the situation they're going to face.

5 **Have fun.** Relax, smile, breathe normally and make eye contact with the audience. Try to enjoy the experience.

These tips apply in almost any situation where a negotiation, discussion or debate is taking place. Your child will benefit hugely from learning these skills early on.

TEAM TASKS

Together with your child, make a list of general 'team roles', for example:

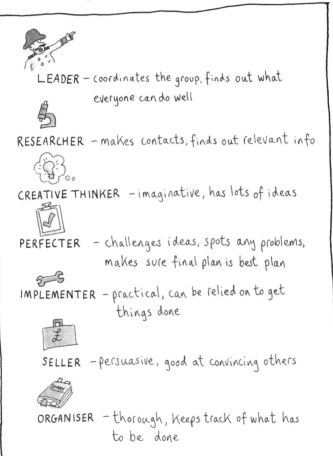

LEADER – coordinates the group, finds out what everyone can do well

RESEARCHER – makes contacts, finds out relevant info

CREATIVE THINKER – imaginative, has lots of ideas

PERFECTER – challenges ideas, spots any problems, makes sure final plan is best plan

IMPLEMENTER – practical, can be relied on to get things done

SELLER – persuasive, good at convincing others

ORGANISER – thorough, keeps track of what has to be done

You may of course give these roles different names.

Encourage your children to engage in team tasks, such as putting on a play for the neighbours, organising a charity event or, when they're older, setting up a mini-business for a week during the holiday – perhaps a dog-walking or car-washing service, or something much more creative, depending on their talents.

Teach your children that the roles on the list above (and any others you can think of) are equally important. Encourage them to try out different roles each time.

SPORTS ANALOGIES

If your children play sports, then they'll have lots of chances to learn about the importance of the team. Your role is to get them to see parallels between their sporting experiences and real life. You could introduce this by chatting about famous sporting quotes, such as:

'The team with the best athletes doesn't usually win. It's the team with the athletes who play best together' – *Lisa Fernandez, softball legend*.

'The way a team plays as a whole determines its success. You may have the greatest bunch of individual stars in the world, but if they don't play together, the club won't be worth a dime' – *Babe Ruth, American baseball player*.

Even if you are on the right track, you'll get run over if you just sit there.

Will Rogers (1879–1935), comedian and social commentator

16 HOW TO DEVELOP INITIATIVE AND FORWARD THINKING

Richard St John spent over a decade interviewing 500 highly successful people from all walks of life in his quest to discover what separates the real high-flyers from the rest. The result? Eight vital ingredients (and a book, *8 to be Great*, 2007).

Most of these ingredients have been covered in the previous chapters: find a passion and love what you do (see Chapter 5), come up with good ideas that will be of value to others (see Chapter 6 and Chapter 7), and work really hard, practise and persist, even through self-doubt and failure (see Chapter 8 and Chapter 10).

In fact, on reflection, they probably sound rather obvious now! And yet these are precisely the sort of almost magical attributes that are far too easy to overlook when our children are being swept along on the tide of tests and doing well at school.

Two more traits on Richard St John's list still need to be addressed, however: 'focus' and 'push'.

If we're going to help our kids to achieve their real potential, then we need to teach them how to push themselves. While some people just seem to be born determined, having a real sense of drive is much more likely to be influenced by how we're brought up. Children need to be helped to see the purpose of their effort, the point of their hard work. My mother, when asked by my teachers what made me so motivated at school, apparently shocked them by replying that she took me round Harrods and showed me all the things I couldn't afford. You may choose not to adopt quite that approach! However, children do need to learn to look ahead and find something to focus on, something they want really badly. And then, once they've found that, they need to know how to go about achieving it.

This may well be one of the most challenging tasks for any parent, so if it proves tricky don't despair! Neuroscience studies have revealed that the area of the brain that deals with forward thinking and planning (the prefrontal cortex) doesn't function fully until early adulthood. It may take a lot of gentle persistence on your part before your child becomes accustomed to the idea of looking further ahead than the following Saturday night.

Nevertheless, we can't avoid the fact that it's up to us to teach our children that their future is in their hands. Successful people believe that they can make things happen – they 'customise' their own lives. So, where do we start? How can we help our children find the track that's right for them and then pursue it successfully? The following tips provide a good place to start.

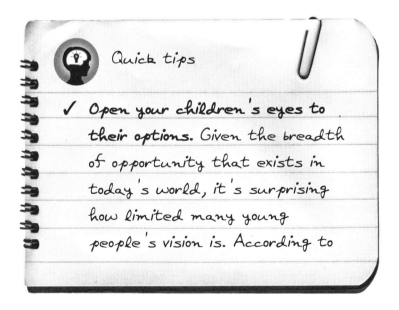

Quick tips

✓ Open your children's eyes to their options. Given the breadth of opportunity that exists in today's world, it's surprising how limited many young people's vision is. According to figures from the Higher Education Statistics Agency (HESA), nearly one in four students fail to complete the degree course they initially began – something that surely indicates how uninformed young people's choices often are. The quality of career guidance in schools varies enormously, and even where you're fortunate and it's great, parents can still play a really useful role in opening their child's eyes to the many different directions they could take. If you can go a step further and help to arrange work experience placements in areas in which your older children have shown an interest, that can be a huge bonus.

✓ **Teach them to set clear goals.** It seems very likely that setting goals is a highly effective way forward. In his bestselling book 'What They Don't Teach You at Harvard Business School', Mark McCormack (1984) describes a study in which a group of MBA students were asked whether they set goals for their future. Just 3 per cent had actually set themselves clear, written goals and plans; 13 per cent had goals in mind but hadn't written them down;

and – as you might expect – 84 per cent hadn't really thought about it. When the researcher followed the students up ten years later, the results were rather astonishing:

- Those who had goals in mind (but not in writing) earned, on average, twice as much as the 84 per cent who had no goals at all.
- Those who had clear written goals earned, on average, ten times as much as the other 97 per cent put together.

Now, for anyone who's suspicious of such studies, you could perhaps argue that it might not be the goals themselves that really made the difference. If you're the type of person who has a vision, who is focused and determined enough to think ahead and work out what you want, then you're probably the type who's more likely going to achieve this. But then, that's exactly what this book is about – helping your child to become that sort of person. And it does seem likely that teaching them to look ahead and set real goals could be a very useful habit to form early. Remember the words of Mary Kay Ash (founder of Mary Kay Cosmetics Inc, voted Most Outstanding Woman in

Business in the Twentieth-Century, 1999): 'An average person with average talents and ambition and average education, can outstrip the most brilliant genius in our society, if that person has clear, focused goals'.

What's more, having goals that are stated clearly may help your child to learn another quality that is essential to success: the ability to self-regulate (otherwise known as putting long-term aims ahead of short-term temptations).

✓ Encourage your child to find out about him- or herself. This may sound a bit trite, but few of us really allow ourselves the luxury to stop and think about who we are and what we truly want from life. And it's just the same for our kids. However, to have the best chance of selecting goals that will make them happy and fulfilled, they need to know themselves. Try to find times to ask your children the big questions and then just listen to their answers, prompting only when necessary. What do they feel are their strengths? What are the things they enjoy most in life? What makes them happy? What do they want out of a career and what are they willing to put into it?

✓ **Give your child plenty of opportunities to take on responsibility and demonstrate initiative.** The saying 'Life is what you make it' is worth remembering. Opportunities rarely fall into our lap – we usually have to create them ourselves. And even when something unexpected comes along, it often takes an enterprising person to recognise what's happened and to act upon it. Your child is more likely to take control of their own life if they've had plenty experience of being

in the driving seat
(metaphorically) while growing
up.

From an early age, try to build
in opportunities for your child
to take responsibility for
things, whether it's packing
their own bag for school,
decorating the table for a
special dinner, looking after a
pet or organising a family
event. And this goes for less
pleasant responsibilities as
well. Sometimes it's very
tempting to step in and take
over, especially if not doing so
means your child has to face
up to some difficult
experiences - but in the longer

term, you're definitely doing
them a favour by holding back.
Don't be a helicopter parent,
hovering too closely overhead
and so preventing your child
from becoming self-sufficient.

✓ **Show that you believe in them
wholeheartedly.** Tell your
child, over and over again and
throughout their life, not just
their childhood, that you
believe in the extraordinary
things that they can achieve
if they put their mind to it
(where, of course,
'extraordinary' is about
fulfilling potential and
needn't mean conventionally
high achieving). Point out their

talents. Remind them of times when they've overcome difficulties or weaknesses. Expectations are powerful things: we live up or down to them. If your child knows in their heart that you believe in them, then they are much more likely to believe in themselves. And that sort of positive attitude will take them a long way …

To quote Mary Kay Ash again: 'Don't limit yourself. Most people limit themselves to what they think they can do. You can go as far as your mind lets you. What you believe, you can achieve.'

Activities and games

You could try ...

FOLLOW MY LEAD

To form an effective plan requires the ability to look ahead, to visualise the steps that will need to be taken, and to articulate these (if only to oneself) in some clear and logical way. A great way of practising these skills with younger children is to start with something familiar.

Children often love making things – from simple cards, masks and models to cakes, sweets and biscuits. Next time your child has learnt to do something, why not set them a challenge – do they think they might be able to teach this to someone else in the family?

If so, encourage them to prepare a list of clear instructions – which could be recorded or written out carefully, depending on age and inclination. Once they are happy with their list and feel confident that they have included all the steps that the other person will need to follow, then it's time to try it out. Your child should read out or play the instructions, pausing where necessary to allow time for their 'pupil' to follow them.

Almost certainly, your child will discover that he or she has left out all sorts of vital pieces of information. Encourage them to think about how their original list could be improved while the activity is taking place. This is a useful exercise that serves to illustrate how much thought and visualisation needs to go into making a really water-tight plan of action. With practice, your child will learn to give much clearer and more detailed instructions – something that is good for their linguistic and planning skills. They'll also get a real kick out of seeing themselves improve – especially if you point this out and praise them along the way.

> ### For the deeper thinker
>
> If your child gets really good at this, you could challenge them to give their instructions without being able to see how their pupil is getting on. This works well over the telephone or by using walkie-talkies. It's really fun for them when their pupil's final product is revealed.

INDEPENDENT PLAY

Help your child to become accustomed, from an early age, to playing and spending some time alone. Banish any fears that you are abandoning your child! By encouraging this, you are helping him or her to become more independent, more creative (in having to entertain him- or herself), more self-sufficient and generally better equipped to deal with a life where we don't always have someone by our side ready to entertain us.

Obviously this needs to be within reason, but as your child gets older you should find that he or she is increasingly able to occupy him- or herself happily. Note that phoning friends and using chatrooms rather defeats the point ...

IN THE CONTROL SEAT

Look out for opportunities when you could give your child control of a particular project. For instance, you could try the following:

- Give your child a patch of garden that they can use to grow whatever they want.
- Allow your child a pet, on the condition that they take on certain responsibilities for it.
- Set a budget and let your child decorate their own bedroom.
- Invite your child to plan an evening when their friends can come round. Their plan should include choosing the menu, buying and cooking the food, etc.
- Let your child have a mobile phone if they can choose the best tariff for their own situation and justify this choice to you.

WALKING ADVENTURES

Teach your children to read maps and to learn to identify the symbols that represent roads, pathways, streams, particular landmarks and different types of vegetation. When you're next thinking about going on a family walk, why not let your kids plan the route? Instead of retracing familiar circuits, it's great fun to sit down with your children beforehand and get them to map out a totally new trail.

Add to their sense of adventure by encouraging them to pack an 'explorer's bag', containing the essentials that they think they'll need for the journey. For instance, they might take food and drink, a compass, a notebook or sketching pad and pencil, a plastic bag to collect (unendangered!) specimens, etc.

Now all you need to do is photocopy the relevant section of the maps so everyone has a copy, and then let your children get on with it. There are bound to be all sorts of occasions when they're not quite sure which direction to take, but this is a great chance to put your heads together and see whether you can work out if there are any key features around you that might provide clues. Pretend that you're baffled too, so that they feel truly in charge – you can easily do this while dropping in hints where necessary so that you don't end up somewhere entirely random.

As your children get more experienced at this, you might consider trying a night walk to listen out for different sounds or a really early morning walk to see the sunrise.

WHAT DO I WANT?

Help your child to get used to setting goals. With younger children, this could be quite a low-key daily activity: in the car on the way to school, for instance, you could ask them what one thing they hope to make happen that day.

As they get a little older, gradually increase the timescale. For instance, on occasional Sundays, you could chat with your child about the four things they really hope they'll achieve during the week ahead. Occasionally, it's worth getting them to write these down, perhaps on separate sticky notes, and asking them to prioritise them using a simple diamond structure:

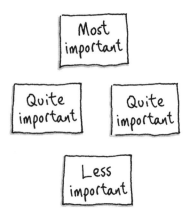

Older children – in their early to mid-teens – could get into the habit of setting annual goals for themselves, perhaps by using the following questions to help them frame these:

- What four things do I want for myself in the coming year?
- What four things do I want for my family?
- What four things do I want for the world?

With the second two categories, encourage them to recognise their own power to make a difference. Are there any seemingly small things they could do that could help towards these goals?

GOOD GOALS

Teach your child how to set 'good goals'. These should:

- **Be specific** – explaining very clearly exactly what they want to achieve.

    'All my life I've wanted to be somebody. But I see now I should have been more specific' – *Jane Wagner, writer and director.*

- **Be manageable** – broken into small, achievable steps.

  'Identify your personal limits and then push past them. Then set new barriers, and repeat the process, again and again and again' – *Nicole Haislett, swimmer, Olympic gold medallist*.

- **Be written down** – this makes them more real.

  'Goals that are not written down are just wishes' – *author unknown*.

- **Be flexible** – sometimes a goal will need to be adapted in the light of what happens.

  'Map out your future, but do it in pencil' – *Jon Bon Jovi, singer*.

- **Have a 'closing date'** – with a deadline to act as an incentive to achieve them.

  'Goals are dreams with deadlines' – *Diana Scharf Hunt, author*.

- **Be rewarded** – by some treat that you and your child set together.

  'The more you praise and celebrate your life, the more there is in life to celebrate' – *Oprah Winfrey, presenter*.

- **Be a life-long process.**

  'You are never too old to set another goal or to dream a new dream' – *C. S. Lewis, author*.

Some people say it's important for our goals to be realistic. But, really, who are we to determine what is a realistic goal for our children? I bet the most successful people had far from realistic goals in mind when they set out – but luckily they didn't listen to anyone who told them this! As Michelangelo said, 'The greatest danger for most of us is not that our aim is too high and we miss it, but that it is too low and we reach it'.

Together with your child, you could make a goal chart for their bedroom wall – with a picture at the end representing the goal your child wants to achieve, and several blank steps getting there that can be filled in gradually. They don't all need to be filled in in advance, as a person's actions often throw up new ideas and requirements for further actions.

The bottom line is that people who know what they want to achieve and who have worked out strategies for getting there have a much better chance of reaching their goals. This is definitely something worth teaching your child.

THINK POSITIVE!

By raising children who know their goals, have plans for how to try to achieve them and know that others believe in them, you are filling them not with blind optimism but with genuinely grounded self-belief.

This ties in with many of the qualities mentioned earlier, such as persistence, risk-taking and resilience – the ability to pick yourself up when you fall, laugh about it, learn from mistakes and move on, always looking for a way in which something good can come from the experience.

Parents can help their children by guiding them through the reflecting process. When something has gone well at school, for instance, chat about the following:

- What did your child actively do to help this happen?
- What role did others/chance play in helping this happen?
- How does this success feel? How can we celebrate it?

When things don't go so well, the experience – though less pleasant – is just as useful (as I described in Chapter 10).

Try to rule out the use of the phrase 'I can't' in your home. Tell your child about the naughty 'internal voice' that whispers negative and pessimistic thoughts in our ears and encourage them to recognise this and to choose to listen to their confident, optimistic voice instead.

MENTAL REHEARSAL

A powerful strategy to help us overcome fears and achieve our goals, mental rehearsal has been shown to have surprisingly convincing results. For instance, some athletes, as well as physically practising a particular movement, will also mentally rehearse each of the steps they need to take to complete the movement successfully. The results are explained by Sarah-Jayne Blakemore (2005) in *The Learning Brain*: '*Mental practice of movement can actually improve muscular strength and movement speed. A recent study showed that people who imagined flexing one of their biceps as hard as possible increased their biceps strength by 13.5% in just a few weeks and maintained that increased strength for several months after stopping the mental exercise.*'

This sort of mental training can also help our children prepare themselves for particular experiences. For example, if your son or daughter has an event coming up that means a lot to them – it may be a talk they have to give in front of their class or a party where they want to make a good impression – then it can help enormously to practise visualising it carefully and clearly beforehand.

By closing your eyes and seeing yourself in a certain context, being aware of what that situation looks and feels like, and then by imagining yourself doing successfully whatever it is that you hope to do, your brain is becoming increasingly familiar with the pattern of actions that you are taking. The pathways literally become stronger – as if you were actually there and doing this in reality.

With your child, taking the first example as an illustration, you could get them to close their eyes and imagine how they feel on the day of their talk. Ask them to imagine getting up, feeling excited, gathering all the necessary things they need to take (being really detailed will help – that's what it's all about), arriving at school, waiting as the others give their talks and controlling their nerves, feeling a little anxious but not listening to the 'worry voice', and feeling mostly excited and in control. Then, standing up, imagine how it looks from the front of the class, seeing all their friends sitting at their desks, seeing the teacher waiting for them to start, and then giving the talk – speaking it through in their mind, imagining using whatever props they plan to involve, and then imagine the clapping at the end, the feeling of relief, the big smile. Do this a few times.

A DAY IN THE LIFE OF …

Few young people have any idea of the huge array of different options that lie before them. When your children are in their early to mid-teens, you could give them a 'future folder', then aim to find out a bit about a different job each fortnight (your child, however enthusiastic about their future, is highly unlikely to be motivated enough to do this alone). Keep this low-key. Remember that it's not meant to be an exercise in influencing them – it's simply to open their eyes to the wealth of opportunities out there. Simply print off a short summary of that job and pass it to them to stick in their folder. There are lots of websites that can help with this.

A final word: forward thinking for parents

My experience tells me that there is no reason to believe that children will acquire the 'secrets of success' described in this book without at least some attention to the conditions and opportunities that are most likely to help them develop. As such, the approach described here really is 'forward thinking for parents', as each chapter has tackled a characteristic or skill that will be of huge benefit to your children, both as they are growing up and, perhaps more importantly, in the future when things become that bit more unpredictable.

We – as parents and teachers – have the opportunity to play an extraordinarily important role in nurturing these qualities. Let's hope that, in doing so, we will help the next generation not only cope with but flourish in times ahead.

BACKGROUND READING

where does this all come from?

I have deliberately chosen not to include too much theory in the main body of this book as it would have made each section much too cumbersome. However, for those of you who are interested in the sources that have contributed to my work over the past years, I include a brief summary of some of the key thinkers in the area.

Blakemore, Sarah-Jayne

As leader of the Developmental Cognitive Neuroscience Group at the Institute of Cognitive Neuroscience, Sarah-Jayne Blakemore has researched widely into social cognition in adolescence. In her book, *The Learning Brain: Lessons for Education* (2005), which she co-authored with Professor Uta Frith, she reviews what is really known about how and when the brain learns and considers the implications of this for educational practice.

Buzan, Tony

One of the most highly recognised authors in the field, Tony Buzan has written extensively on effective learning and memory strategies and is the creator of Mind Maps®, a powerful tool that has helped people and businesses across the world. Of his many books, *Brain Child: How Smart Parents Make Smart Kids* (2003), *Mind Maps for Kids: An Introduction* (2003) and *The Buzan Study Skills Handbook* (2006) are all particularly recommended as practical, accessible resources for parents.

Claxton, Guy

Currently Co-Director of the Centre for Real-World Learning and Professor of the Learning Sciences at the University of Winchester, Guy Claxton has been a leading campaigner for change in schools for many years. His programme 'Building Learning Power' supports schools in helping young people to become more independent and creative in their own approach to learning – developing skills that will help them survive and succeed beyond school. For a powerful description of the problems with modern-day schooling, try his book, *What's the Point of School? Rediscovering the Heart of Education* (2008).

Costa, Arthur

Co-Director of the Institute for Intelligent Behavior in California, Arthur Costa is a leading educationalist in the USA. In describing 16 'habits of mind' that range from 'persisting' and 'managing impulsivity' to 'taking responsible risks' and 'striving for accuracy', he created (together with Bena Kallick) an exciting new way of defining what is important in education.

Dweck, Carol

A Professor at Stanford University, Carol Dweck has carried out extensive research in the field of motivation, personality and development. Her work is highly influential and has major implications for the way we bring up and teach young people. Her key point is that some individuals have a 'fixed' theory of intelligence (believing that success is based on innate ability) whereas others hold a 'growth' theory (recognising that success is based on hard work and learning). The results of these two fundamentally different mindsets are significant, particularly in how they affect a person's response to set-backs and failure. A fascinating description of this can be found in *Mindset: The New Psychology of Success* (2006).

Gardner, Howard

The creator of Multiple Intelligence Theory, Howard Gardner is Hobbs Professor of Cognition and Education at the Harvard Graduate School of Education. His proposal, back in 1983, was that the traditional way in which intelligence is defined is far too narrow, failing to embrace alternative kinds of intelligence such as musical, bodily and interpersonal intelligences. This suggests that students could benefit if teachers use a wider variety of approaches to reach them and tap into their abilities.

Gladwell, Malcolm

Journalist and author of three international best-sellers – *The Tipping Point* (2000), *Blink* (2005) and, most recently,

Outliers: The Story of Success (2008) – Malcolm Gladwell just seems to have his finger on the pulse when it comes to exposing patterns of behaviour and their implications. In *Outliers*, he examines how a person's environment affects his or her possibility and opportunity for success, illustrating this with several fascinating case studies.

Perkins, David

A Senior Professor of Education at the Harvard Graduate School of Education, David Perkins has conducted extensive research in the field of teaching and learning for understanding, creativity, problem-solving and reasoning in the arts, sciences and everyday life. He co-directed Harvard's Project Zero for 25 years, exploring practical interventions that schools can take to develop meaningful learning that promotes active thinking and understanding.

Robinson, Ken

Sir Ken Robinson is an internationally recognised leader in the development of creativity, innovation and human resources. Having worked with governments, international agencies and some of the world's leading companies, he wrote *Out of Our Minds: Learning to be Creative* (2001) to expose the damaging discrepancy between what businesses need – people who are creative, innovative and flexible – and what schools and society are providing. He argues that radical changes are needed in the way we think about our own intelligence and creativity and in how we should educate our children to meet the challenges of living and working in the twenty-first century.

Sternberg, Robert

Another key figure in the debate about intelligence is Robert Sternberg of Yale University. Arguing that IQ is an inadequate definition, he conceived 'successful intelligence' – the ability to capitalise on one's strengths and correct or compensate for one's weaknesses through a balance of analytical, creative and practical abilities. More simply, what matters is how a person responds, how they think, how they weigh up different interests and how they act.

References

Introduction

de Botton, A. (2000) *The Consolations of Philosophy*. New York: Pantheon.

Dweck, C. S. (2000) *Self-theories: Their Role in Motivation, Personality and Development*. Philadelphia: Psychology Press, Taylor & Francis.

Gladwell, M. (2008) *Outliers: The Story of Success*. New York: Little, Brown.

Robinson, K. (2001) *Out of Our Minds: Learning to be Creative*. Oxford: Capstone.

Tahir, T. (2008) 'Why we can't turn our backs on the league table generation', *Times Higher Education*, 10 January 2008.

1 How to stimulate independent thinking

Gilbert, I. (2007) *The Little Book of Thunks*. Carmarthen: Crown House.

Law, S. (2000) *The Philosophy Files*. London: Orion Children's Books.

Shepherd, J. (2007) 'I think, therefore I earn', *The Guardian*, 20 November 2007.

2 How to grow a vivid imagination

Danks, F. and Schofield, J. (2005) *Nature's Playground*. London: Frances Lincoln.

Johnson, S. (2005) *Everything Bad is Good for You: How Today's Popular Culture is Actually Making Us Smarter*. New York: Riverhead Books.

4 How to kindle a burning curiosity

Claxton, G. (2002) *Building Learning Power*. Bristol: TLO Limited.

5 How to develop a 'let's find out' approach

Buzan, T. (2003) *Mind Maps for Kids: An Introduction*. London: HarperCollins.

6 How to encourage originality and creativity

von Oech, R. (1998) *A Whack on the Side of the Head*. New York: Warner Books.

Gladwell, M. (2008) *Outliers: The Story of Success*. New York: Little, Brown.

7 How to become innovative and inventive

Bridge, R. (2006) *My Big Idea*. London: Kogan Page.

Claxton, G. (1997) *Hare Brain, Tortoise Mind: Why Intelligence Increases When You Think Less*. London: Fourth Estate.

8 How to discover the magic of persistence

Claxton, G. (2002) *Building Learning Power*. Bristol: TLO Limited.

Cowell, S. (2003) *I Don't Mean to Be Rude, But...* London: Ebury Press.

Gladwell, M. (2008) *Outliers: The Story of Success*. New York: Little, Brown.

The New Yorker (2003) 'Medical superman?', **www.anecdotage.com/index.php?aid=15841**

Zeleznock, T. (2008) '7 entrepreneurs whose perseverance will inspire you', **www.growthink.com/content/7-entrepreneurs-whose-perseverance-will-inspire-you**

9 How to take the right sort of risk

Bennett, R. (2008) 'Children need risk to thrive as adults, says Dragons' Den judge', *The Times*, 10 July 2008.

Frean, A. (2008) 'Local authorities challenged with bid to have children play outside', *The Times*, 4 April 2008.

12 How to think flexibly

Dawson, H. (2007) 'Thriving in a faster world', **www.praesta.co.uk/news/pressreleases/article/i65767773.html**

13 How to make wise decisions

Claxton, G. (2008) *What's the Point of School?* Richmond: One World.

14 How to enjoy solving problems

de Bono, E. (1969) *The Mechanism of Mind*. New York: Simon & Schuster.

von Oech, R. (1998) *A Whack on the Side of the Head*. New York: Warner Books.

15 How to have social savvy

Gardner, H. (2006) *Five Minds for the Future*. Boston: Harvard Business School Press.

Gladwell, M. (2008) *Outliers: The Story of Success*. New York: Little, Brown.

Pullman, P. (1995) *Northern Lights*. London: Scholastic.

16 How to develop initiative and forward thinking

Blakemore, S. J. and Frith, U. (2005) *The Learning Brain: Lessons for Education*. Oxford: Blackwell.

McCormack, M. H. (1984) *What They Don't Teach You at Harvard Business School*. Toronto: Bantam Books.

St John, R. (2007) *8 to be Great*. Toronto: Train of Thought Arts.

Background reading

Blakemore, S. J. and Frith, U. (2005) *The Learning Brain: Lessons for Education*. Oxford: Blackwell.

Buzan, T. (2003) *Brain Child: How Smart Parents Make Smart Kids*. London: HarperCollins.

Buzan, T. (2003) *Mind Maps for Kids: An Introduction*. London: HarperCollins.

Buzan, T. (2006) *The Buzan Study Skills Handbook*. London: BBC Active.

Claxton, G. (2008) *What's the Point of School?* Richmond: One World.

Dweck, C. (2006) *Mindset: The New Psychology of Success*. New York: Random House.

Gladwell, M. (2000) *The Tipping Point*. Boston: Little, Brown.

Gladwell, M. (2005) *Blink*. New York: Little, Brown.

Gladwell, M. (2008) *Outliers: The Story of Success*. New York: Little, Brown.

Robinson, K. (2001) *Out of Our Minds: Learning to be Creative*. Oxford: Capstone.